SpringerBriefs in Economics

Volume 89

SpringerBriefs present concise summaries of cutting-edge research and practical applications across a wide spectrum of fields. Featuring compact volumes of 50 to 125 pages, the series covers a range of content from professional to academic. Typical topics might include:

- A timely report of state-of-the art analytical techniques
- A bridge between new research results, as published in journal articles, and a contextual literature review
- A snapshot of a hot or emerging topic
- An in-depth case study or clinical example
- A presentation of core concepts that students must understand in order to make independent contributions

SpringerBriefs in Economics showcase emerging theory, empirical research, and practical application in microeconomics, macroeconomics, economic policy, public finance, econometrics, regional science, and related fields, from a global author community.

Briefs are characterized by fast, global electronic dissemination, standard publishing contracts, standardized manuscript preparation and formatting guidelines, and expedited production schedules.

More information about this series at http://www.springer.com/series/8876

Jürgen Georg Backhaus
Editor

The University According to Humboldt

History, Policy, and Future Possibilities

Springer

Editor
Jürgen Georg Backhaus
Krupp Foundation Chair in Public Finance
and Fiscal Sociology
University of Erfurt
Erfurt
Germany

ISSN 2191-5504 ISSN 2191-5512 (electronic)
SpringerBriefs in Economics
ISBN 978-3-319-13855-8 ISBN 978-3-319-13856-5 (eBook)
DOI 10.1007/978-3-319-13856-5

Library of Congress Control Number: 2015930831

Springer Cham Heidelberg New York Dordrecht London

Printed on acid-free paper

Springer is a brand of Springer International Publishing
Springer International Publishing is part of Springer Science+Business Media (www.springer.com)

Introduction

The University According to Humboldt and the Alternatives

Introduction

The *Liberation of the Serfs*[1] and *The University according to Humboldt and the Alternatives* were, respectively, topics for Heilbronn symposia.

Wilhelm von Humboldt, of course, reformed a very old pan-German institution, these reforms provide a legacy and, as such, also hints for the future.

The Heilbronn Symposia in Economics and the Social Sciences always take up a topic embedded in the German language, examine it carefully from all sides in English, and try to distill lessons for the future.

We would like to thank the Lord Mayor and the city council of the city of Heilbronn for their continuous support.

Universität Erfurt Prof. Dr. Dr. h.c. Jürgen Backhaus

[1] Jürgen G. Backhaus (ed.): The Liberation of the Serfs—The Economics of Unfree Labor, New York: Springer, 2012.

Contents

The University Before Humboldt and After

Jürgen Backhaus

This piece is dedicated to my dear friend Moni, who left the room once I had started and returned only after I was finished. I should have told her, that it was a short piece, then she would have given another proof of her patience with me.

I. In this article, I want to explore the alternatives to the picture of the university Humboldt presented. Obviously, there was a counter picture, because Humboldt's reforms needed something that was to be reformed. Take the University of Erfurt, which was founded in 1378 and which Humboldt dissolved in 1816, as there were only half as many students as professors at the time. The university he closed was one of the oldest in Germany, founded in 1378, and it is an experience that is primetime in the early renaissance, with Luther for instance proclaiming, if you want to study well, study in Erfurt. Paracelsus had studied in Perugia, one of the oldest European Universities, and he was appointed a professor at the city of Basel, as no university would tolerate his teachings and his abominable Latin. This gives us a hint to university reform looking back, as teaching was also made possible at the university level outside the university. Note this as point 1.

II. The traditional university also had its own income revenue. This was largely achieved by giving traditional church and monastery revenues to the new universities; a good example is Marburg on the Lahn River. The university is also provided by fees. For instance, Marx earned his doctorate from the University of Jena by paying a fee to the dean. He never appeared for a defense. The universities, composed of students and professors, were thoroughly self-managed institutions, professors and students could be elected as rectors. The University of Erfurt for instance had Amplonius as a student rector, later as a professor rector, he was a physician, and then later a major donor of his precious library. He served as the physician of the archbishop of Cologne and was obviously well paid, since he assembled a very precious library of some 600 scripts which he later donated to the University of Erfurt. Upon his death, a

J. Backhaus (✉)
Faculty of Economics, Law and Social Sciences, Krupp Foundation Chair in Public Finance and Fiscal Sociology, University of Erfurt, Nordhäuser Str. 63, 99089 Erfurt, Germany
e-mail: juergen.backhaus@uni-erfurt.de

J. G. Backhaus (ed.), *The University According to Humboldt*,
SpringerBriefs in Economics 89, DOI 10.1007/978-3-319-13856-5_1

war ensued between the archdiocese of Cologne and the city of Erfurt over the library. What a happier reason to fight a war. The city of Erfurt prevailed, and Erfurt prevailed again in 1955, when the library was returned from Russia to Erfurt almost intact. Stalin could not control Latin speakers, and for that reason nobody revealed his ability of speaking Latin for fear of being killed. In this way, no use could be made of it in Stalin-controlled Russia, and the library was returned and is now part of the library system of the University of Erfurt.

III. It should be pointed out that professorial performance is of course tied to remuneration. In Erfurt, professors were paid for instance by beer brewing licenses. It is no surprise that for a good Erfurt professor it was wise to marry an inkeeper's daughter who knew how to use these licenses. Hence, with long iterations, it is no surprise that Erfurt professors were particularly found in their wives' inns, rather than in the lecture hall, drinking beer with the few students remaining. On the contrary, in Jena, professors lived on the income of the house, as they charged for room and board and use of the library. Hence, professors were got to marrying widows with large libraries that their husbands had bequeathed to them. If under these incentives systems you run two universities next to each other for a long time, you find excellence next to nebulance.

IV. Several years ago, my teacher Bruno Frey with Rainer Eichenberger launched the idea of functionally organized competing jurisdictions (Frey and Eichenberger 1999). It strikes me as a perfect example of the pre-Humboldt university to describe them as functionally organized competing jurisdictions.
The idea of functionally organized competing jurisdictions fits the traditional university that Humboldt abolished, well. The university was a public institution by its own right with citizens as students and professors. Sometimes, we find reminiscence in that some university bestows the honor of an honorary citizen (Ehrenbürger) instead of for instance an honorary doctors degree or an honorary professorship.

V. What is it that the traditional university before Humboldt holds in this age of Bologna? In my opinion, there are at least three points. First, universities should have their own sources of funding. Second, it is a graceful idea to grant universities the status of semi-states, where students and professors enjoy citizenship which they can transfer in all areas of the Bologna treaty. This would greatly enhance flexibility within the system. Third, granting universities their juridical independence from states and make them states within the states strikes me as a promising prospect.[1]

In this short essay, I have outlined that Humboldt's university reform was not without an alternative, rather obviously, but that the traditional university indeed could serve as a model for a university within the Bologna process.

[1] Incidentally, this is a demand of Rudolf Steiner (Steiner 1919), who sees such university independence from the state as the solution of the Social Question.

References

Frey, B. S. & Eichenberger, R. (1999). *The New Democratic Federalism for Europe. Functional, Overlapping and Competing Jurisdictions*. Cheltenham: Edward Elgar.

Steiner, R. (1919). Die Kernpunkte der sozialen Frage. (The Crucial Points of the Social Question) Rudolf Steiner Online Archiv 4th ed. 2010. http://anthroposophie.byu.edu/schriften/023.pdf. Accessed 7 May 2015.

The University According to Humboldt and the Alternatives

Jürgen Backhaus

When Wilhelm von Humboldt reformed the Prussian universities, at the same time he increased the number and enrollment of these universities substantially, yet he also closed the University of Erfurt, which had seen its prime during the Middle Ages and has only been refounded in our days in a second attempt in 1994. In this sense, the University of Erfurt provides a wonderful example to discuss not only Humboldt's reform and the alternatives, but at the same time, in looking at the time before and after Humboldt, we can see the alternatives in terms of first what he had found and found in need of reform, and second which challenges should now be considered also in a comparative perspective.

Currently, we still live in America's century which may be coming to an end; nevertheless, the American example always needs to be considered alongside. Although the university in the sense of a graduate school was imported to the USA from Germany, currently the music clearly plays in the USA as far as advanced scholarship is concerned. The basic American university, however, contrary to the Humboldt ideal has three instead of two functions: education, research, and extension. The extended university is much better networked in its community than the European one, and this has important repercussions for its financial viability.

When the University of Erfurt was refounded, the then chancellor Dr. Helmut Kohl had tried to refound it as a university of foundations. However, the climate for foundations and donations in Germany proved to be still sterile, when once it had thrived. The chancellor succeeded in securing just one chair (my own). This would have been inconceivable for an extended university such as an American one. As university finances continue to be difficult, sometimes outright precarious, it is therefore sensible to think in terms of the extended university also in the European context.

J. Backhaus (✉)
Faculty of Economics, Law, and Social Sciences, Krupp Foundation Chair in Public Finance and Fiscal Sociology, University of Erfurt, Nordhäuser Str. 63, 99089 Erfurt, Germany
e-mail: juergen.backhaus@uni-erfurt.de

J. G. Backhaus (ed.), *The University According to Humboldt*,
SpringerBriefs in Economics 89, DOI 10.1007/978-3-319-13856-5_2

This paper has a straightforward structure. In starting briefly from the Humboldt reform as such, in part two I look back at the medieval university and then, in part three, I consider the university in its future perspectives also from an international point of view.

1

When Humboldt set out with his reforms of higher education, this was of course in the context of all the Napoleonic and post-Napoleonic reforms in Prussia, and after the Congress of Vienna, Prussia had re-emerged and enlarged but was also heavily in debt. The University of Erfurt proved to be resistible to any reform attempt and was therefore closed. The privileges of the university were, however, transferred to Breslau, which was along with Königsberg much strengthened. He also founded, of course, the University "Unter den Linden" in Berlin.

The university in the medieval system was before the advent of the national state something like a state within the state. The members of the university, students, and professors, were citizens with their own rights and privileges, the rector and the deans would not only confer degrees, but the rector, for instance, could also legitimize illegitimate children.

Wilhelm von Humboldt was working in the context of an emerging nation state and therefore did away with these peculiar privileges of semi-statehood. Instead, the universities were constructed as public authorities within the civil service but with the specific professorial privileges, freedom of research, and instruction. The students had likewise enjoyed full university system privileges, but now they were users of a public institution (Anstalt) and subject to the bylaws of this institution (Anstaltsordnung). When during the 1960s of the twentieth century students demanded participation rights in the universities, they apparently did not recall they could have much more effectively insisted on their ancient rights instead of demanding something new: "Unter den Talaren Muff von tausend Jahren" ("Under the gowns a thousand years of stuffiness") was their slogan which revealed ignorance of history.

Importantly, the financial conditions of the universities were also reformed and put on a regular basis. The medieval university had known sometimes bizarre financial conditions. In Erfurt, for instance, you can still see next to the doors of old university professors' houses a cavity where a broom fits. Here a broom would show when the professor enjoyed the day of brewing. Professors at the University of Erfurt were largely paid in brewing rights, and for this reason it was sensible for them to marry an innkeeper's daughter. In Jena, on the other hand, which after all is a much more recent university, such privileges were not known. Instead, the professorial household lived on lodging the students who could also use the professor's library. For this reason, a professor would sensibly marry a professor's widow who had also inherited her husband's library; hence, he could not only use the library but also benefit from a well-managed professorial household.

If professors are recruited in this manner for centuries, it can come as no surprise that ultimately the University of Jena would thrive and the University of Erfurt had to be closed. Indeed, when the University of Erfurt was closed, there were twice as many professors there as students, and they tended to be found in their inns rather than the lecturing halls.

Other universities, such as the University of Marburg, had agricultural revenues at their disposal. Philipp of Hesse, the reformer, had simply closed a monastery and turned over its rich estates to the university. The livelihood of the university now depended on agricultural vicissitudes. The professors had certain quantities of wood and wine for their livelihood as well as, of course, the lecture fees.

2

The history of the pre-Humboldt university is best divided into two phases, roughly the period before and including Paracelsus, i.e. Philippus Theophrastus Aureolus Bombastus von Hohenheim, and the post-reform counter-reformation and counter-counter-reformation universities before Humboldt. While scholarly learning in the Middle Ages had mostly thrived in the monasteries, the universities really began to blossom when the scholars arrived from Constantinople with their libraries and universities were founded in upper Italy. Paracelsus had studied in Perugia and he later became a professor in the city of Basel and not at the university, where he was not tolerated. Paracelsus was a wandering scholar, the founder of scholarly pharmacy and also the founder of a specialized type of medicine devoted to treating work-related injuries and conditions. Labour practices particularly in mining were in such demand that the need for such a specialized practice of medicine was simply undeniable. The advent of the reformation brought a wave of university foundations, often monasteries were transformed into universities lock, stock, and barrel. The University of Marburg provides just such an example. The reformation, of course, was an ongoing process. The University of Erfurt received many professors from Prague, the oldest German university, as the beginning reformation which in Bohemia also was a nationalist movement forced the professors to go elsewhere. Previously, Erfurt primarily had contacts with the Sorbonne. An instrument of reformation was also the University of Groningen in the north of the Netherlands. In the beginning, this university did not have a single Dutch professor, all the professors came from Germany. The reformation also gave rise to the University of Herborn, where Johannes Althusius taught who later became the syndic of Emden, an important port city. In the case of Althusius, religion, public law, and the sciences of state are just one amalgam (Althusius 1995).

The counter-reformation gave rise to university foundations, again, however, under rather different auspices. The University of Würzburg provides a fine example. Here, the professors were explicitly barred from publishing. The city, of course, also has an excellent vineyard, and Lujo Brentano still provides a colorful account of studying there. As he had a girlfriend there, Lujo Brentano had decided to study in Würzburg, and he tells of a lecture in public finance: "There were three students next to the professor, first one neighbor fell asleep, then the other. When I woke up, the professor was sound asleep" (Brentano 2009).

Sometimes there were even counter-counter-reformations, notably when former church territories due to the Napoleonic reforms and the Congress of Vienna became secular. The most important reforms, however, were those by Friedrich Althoff in the late nineteenth century (Backhaus 1993). This was, of course, a post-Humboldt reform, certainly not less forceful. The empire (Reich) now had 25 constituent states, Prussia was the biggest and the Reichslande (imperial lands) Elsass-Lothringen had the University of Strasbourg. Incidentally, the Althoff reforms comprised the Prussian universities, Strasbourg and also the universities in Baden, as the grand duchy of Baden moved in tandem with Prussia on university affairs.

During Althoffs's administration, the universities in Prussia doubled in terms of number, enrolment and professorial staff. With respect to financial arrangements, Althoff was indeed ingenious. The University of Frankfurt was a university entirely made up of foundations. The same was true for the Emperor William Foundation, a research wing added to the university system. Major donors were count Henkel von Donnersmarck from Silesia and the Rothschild widow.

The University of Frankfurt was also an important outlet for racial pressure. The many Jewish university teachers who could not be accommodated in either Austria or Bavaria found employment there, the same was true for the University of Strasbourg.

As in the case of Georg Simmel, sometimes the family founded a chair to which the appointee would be named. Althoff was also responsible for the creation of entire new disciplines and academic disciplines, for instance business economics. In order to appease the Westphalians (for the loss of their kingdom and being made part of Prussia), the Wilhelms University would be located in Munster. Similarly, a technical university was founded in Aachen, and technical universities also received the ius promovendi against stiff opposition from traditional quarters; this is why the doctor in technical sciences is written in German and therefore with a capital "I" (Dr. Ing.). This was the only compromise, otherwise the technical universities were made totally equal to the traditional universities.

The Althoff system had been discussed at a different conference in 1989, which is why we now turn to part III.

3

At present, the most pressing demand facing the traditional universities in Germany is the quest for the ius promovendi by the universities of applied sciences. Probably, the best that can be done here from the point of view of overall academic performance is to offer little resistance as such but stiff resistance to laxness and negligence in standards.

Althoff introduced a written dissertation, which was then also required in Heidelberg. Consequently, American students who wanted to graduate but could not or did not wish to submit a written dissertation went to Leipzig in Saxony. Likewise, universities of applied sciences should not be allowed to give away the doctorate or grant it for applied work, the doctorate should remain to be reserved for basic research. As this will be initially difficult to master for many but not all professors at universities of applied sciences, those will look for help to professors at universities. Often, professors at universities of applied sciences are actually would-be university professors who could not find an appointment there. With much difficulty, but often the cooperation of the Ministry of Education, the requirements for practical experience can be finessed in such cases, and as far as these professors are concerned, often having passed the requirements for the habilitation (in America second dissertation), the problem is virtually nonexistent.

In the future, the independence of universities and university funding will have to be addressed as the prime objectives of science policy. In this context, we should also note that the right to found private universities and to insist on a license to be granted by the state is really an important precondition for university independence and sanity. Of course, with 16 federal states, there is a modicum of competition between them, and this modicum of competition is, of course, a guarantor for some freedom. But the right of the citizen to enjoy freedom of research and education also extends to the right of founding universities and having them certified when they fulfill nonarbitrary requirements. This is important from the point of view of content of (teaching and research) for both teachers and students, as in the Middle Ages. But it is also important from the point of view of saving universities from financial strangulation with the intent of accomplishing rather material ends. In our time, we witness that a Prime Minister of a German federal state (North Rhine-Westphalia) gave in to popular demands and in one night founded five universities. Although substantial advances were made to fund these universities, what could be accomplished was certainly impressive but probably not enough. Today, we face the bizarre spectacle that one of these universities has been closed, one entire university budget has been struck from the state budget, yet we do not know which university this is, as all five of them still continue to exist—the resistance to closing one down from the local communities proved insurmountable to the state government. Such a situation is obviously not just bizarre, it is testimony to the unsatisfactory situation at which universities exist if they can only rely on the public for funding.

For this reason, in the future we will increasingly have to look for the alternative of a private extended university. Clear enough, the extended university in the American context is typically a public one. One third of the unsettled land (from which mostly Indians were driven) was set aside for the development of churches and universities. These universities would then be located in remote areas, and the land would only increase in value when the establishment thrived. Yet, the American context always allows for exceptions, Cornell, for instance, is a university that is both private and land-grant. The extended university is typically so interwoven with its extension, i.e. whatever extends beyond, that it is next to inconceivable that it would lack the resources for its own development. Agriculture, the neighborhoods and the cities around it are so dependent on this university as an institution that provides education during the day and in the evening, consultation of all kinds but also facilities such as airports, that the extended university never fails to meet the demand that can also pay for its sustenance. In recent years, many state governments have probed means to grant universities more independence, typically with a view to also loosening their grip on the state's budget. Typically, these are entitlements and the state can do nothing but discourage the use of them. The most drastic but also most helpful way for state governments to grant universities more independence is at the same time a very painless one. It is simply to grant them the ability to find a status as an extended university.

References

Althusius, J. (1995). *Politica. An abridged translation of politics methodically set forth and illustrated with sacred and profane examples* (ed. and trans: F. S. Carney. Foreword by D. J. Elazar). Indianapolis: Liberty Fund.

Backhaus, J. (Ed.) (1993). *The economics of science policy. An analysis of the Althoff system*. MCB University Press (Journal of Economic Studies. Vol. 20, No. 4/5, 1993). Bingley: Emerald Group Publishing.

Brentano, L. (2009). Elsässer Erinnerungen, Berlin: Erich Reiß Verlag.

The Lexicographical Utility Function of Fertility Decisions and Humboldt's Political Principles of the State

Gerhard Scheuerer

1 Introduction

Policy in developed as well as developing countries takes measures to influence more or less the reproduction behavior. Extents of manipulation depend particularly with regard to cultural, ancient, and moral concepts of the country and its Government. In the mind of Wilhelm von Humboldt (Humboldt (1991)—see paragraph 3.), education and liberty are first and essential sine qua non from a theoretical point of view arranging political activities. In consideration of Humboldt's principles of the state, the aim of this essay is to contribute to solutions of basic problems and difficulties of today prevailing Theory of the Family. As far as obvious, there exist economic investigations about the influence of only a few variables. These partial analytical investigations deal with explanatory variables like the level of education, duration of education, income of men and women, and allocation of time within the family. Other variables in those studies are treated as external variables (Althammer (2000), p 55 ff. as well as p. 115). By consequence, the existing models on the basis of empirical data are restricted models as one author aptly puts it "...the programming models mostly used in this context become very quickly so complicated that they are scarcely usable and results cannot be deduced obviously" (Lechner 1998, p. 472). Cigno points out this very clearly: "The relatively few attempts at constructing such a model are based on drastic simplifications that remove much of the economic content. ...Furthermore, these models tell us nothing about how actual or expected birth control is affected by differences in personal characteristics, or by changes in the economic environment" (Cigno 1991, p. 127). In times of unimaginable IT memory, there must be taken efforts to shorten this lack of

G. Scheuerer (✉)
Faculty of Economics, Law, and Social Sciences, University of Erfurt, PO Box 90 02 21, 99089 Erfurt, Germany
e-mail: gerhard-scheuerer@t-online.de

J. G. Backhaus (ed.), *The University According to Humboldt*,
SpringerBriefs in Economics 89, DOI 10.1007/978-3-319-13856-5_3

econometric models. On the other hand, there is a lack of comprehensive family and fertility models. Existing models cannot explain the whole plethora of dependent variables. Therefore, actual family policy in many countries and especially in Germany walks in the dark, because there are not enough theoretical models combining the entire number of variables to make reasonable estimates on the basis of available data.

This essay tries to establish some middle ground between radical empiricism and method-guided econometrics. With this attempt 27 variables are described which influence population development and reproduction behavior. Empirical methodological surveys would be very important to establish, concerning the actual drastic population development to remove wrong economic incentives especially as far as economic policy, tax policy, and pension policy are concerned. Family policy could be qualified on that basis.

The essay wants to help to come back to a complete look at empirically founded variables of population development and fertility. Analyses of the demographic situation in united Germany seem to be favorable for recognizing dependences because they occur more clearly in changing transformation processes. Therefore, this essay deals with the development of the population of Thuringia, a federal state in the Federal Republic of Germany, by way of example. The investigation focuses on demographical changes since turnaround in late 1980s. It is based on empirical data and the Economics of the Family and tries to combine different explanations about the variables that influence fertility (Becker 1981, 1986; Becker and Murphy 2000; Becker and Posner 2009; McKenzie and Tullock 1984; Althammer 2000; Caldwell and Schindlmayr 2003; de Bruijn 2005; Dondrich 2007).

2 Empirical Analysis of Demographic Developments

In the following, four categories of parameters influencing reproduction behavior and population development are distinguished (Scheuerer 2010, pp. 147–223).

Basic Thesis Economic and social conditions as well as citizens' behavior change over a long period. These alterations lead to changing reproduction behavior.

2.1 Statistical Demographic Variables

First Thesis The size of the current population as well as its structure is the result of fertility, mortality, and mobility developments in the past (population effect).

The number of persons living in the federal state of Thuringia and its preceding districts declined from 2,785,079 in 1956 to 2,235,025 in the year 2010. That amounts to 19.8 % in 54 years. The number of men declined 11.6 %, the number of women declined 26.4 % (Table 1).

Table 1 Population development in Thuringia 1956–2010. (Source: Thuringian State Statistical Office: Statistical yearbooks)

Year	Population		
	Total	Men	Women
1956	2,785,079	1,248,916	1,536,163
1960	2,737,865	1,237,121	1,500,744
1965	2,747,767	1,262,229	1,485,538
1970	2,759,084	1,279,965	1,479,119
1975	2,737,235	1,280,548	1,456,687
1980	2,730,368	1,289,813	1,443,555
1985	2,721,539	1,292,132	1,429,407
1989	2,683,877	1,286,720	1,397,157
1992	2,545,808	1,224,415	1,321,393
1995	2,503,785	1,214,213	1,289,572
2000	2,431,255	1,189,951	1,241,304
2002	2,392,040	1,174,211	1,217,829
2003	2,373,157	1,166,263	1,206,894
2005	2,334,575	1,149,515	1,185,060
2008	2,267,763	1,118,827	1,148,936
2010	2,235,025	1,103,693	1,131,332

Second Thesis Changed gender proportion influences opportunities for periodic and cohort fertility (structural effect).

As consequence of long-run population developments, the gender proportion changed to more men and fewer women. From 1980 to 1989, the proportion of men and women in the fertility age of 15–45 years old has been nearly 97 women per 100 men; up to 2010 this changed to 88 women per 100 men (Table 2). The opportunities for fertility of the population sank rapidly since transformation 1989.

Table 2 Population development in the age of 15–45 years from 1980 to 2010. (Source: Thuringian State Statistical Office: Statistical yearbooks)

Year	Population			Women per 100 men
	Total	Men	Women	
1980	1,242,981	631,888	611,093	96.7
1985	1,220,278	619,766	600,512	96.7
1989	1,170,617	598,471	572,146	95.6
1992	1,107,312	568,386	538,926	94.8
1995	1,122,264	581,875	540,389	92.9
2000	1,038,678	545,060	493,618	90.6
2002	1,007,210	530,751	476,459	89.7
2005	946,850	500,605	446,245	89.1
2008	833,421	441,776	391,645	88.6
2010	769,847	408,864	360,983	88.3

Third Thesis Compared with natural population development, mobility becomes an increasing influence on cohort fertility. Structural effects overrun population effect.

Today, both size and structure of the Thuringian population are result of a long-run development in the twentieth century, particularly of a decline in fertility and increase of life expectance since the end of the nineteenth century, a crisis perceived as a worldwide economic crisis in the 1930s, people killed during World War I and II, expulsion following World War II, escape from the dictatorship in the German Democratic Republic (GDR), construction of the wall around the GDR in 1961 and emigration to West Germany since 1989 under always unusual and challenging circumstances.

In the time span between 1992 and 2010, the population declined by slightly more than 14,000 persons per year. In 2010, 55 % were attributed to the surplus of people who had died over children born and 45 % to the surplus of emigration over immigration (Table 3). This average proportion changed for example up to the year 2002, and in that year the figures were 46.5–53.5 %. Up to mid-2000 the emigrations share in the population decline of Thuringia exceeded death. Furthermore, Thuringia loses ten children per day by abortion nowadays.

Fourth Thesis Public benefits influence only periodic fertility. Concerning cohort fertility, they fail in the long run and lead to scheduling of births planned for later.

Since 1950, with the exception of several years in the decades of 1970 and 1980, the development of periodic total fertility was very similar in West Germany and East Germany. The exception was due to the policy of population development of the GDR, which however failed in the long run. The people took benefits, but did not raise their fertility rate for long and the cohort fertility sank continuously (Table 4). The periodic birth rates grew up only for some years because of scheduling birth originally planned for later. The periodic total fertility was in Thuringia in 1989 with 1537.3 born children per 1000 women in the age of 15–45 years 10 %

Table 3 Population development in Thuringia 2009. (Source: Thuringian State Statistical Office: Statistical yearbook 2010, own calculation)

Population development	Persons	
	Absolute	Per day
Natural:		
Birth	16,854	46.2
Death	−26,774	−73.4
Balance	−9920	−27.2
Territorial:		
Immigration	34,732	95.2
Emigration	−42,758	−117.1
Balance	−8026	−22.0
Total balance of population development	−17,946	−49.2
Further population deficit		
Abortion	−3797	−10.4

Table 4 Cohort fertilities of women born in the years 1950, 1955–1983 in Thuringia. (Source of data: Thuringian State Statistical Office: Statistical yearbooks, own calculation)

Year of birth	CTFR	Year of birth	CTFR	Year of birth	CTFR
1950	1861.0	1959	1941.7	1963	1673.8
1955	1929.0	1960	1906.3	1964	1609.3
1956	1948.0	1961	1897.6	1965	1585.7
1957	1936.6	1962	1795.3	1966	1534.8
1958	1955.5				
Year of birth	CTFR < 32	Year of birth	CTFR < 32	Year of birth	CTFR < 32
1950	1744.0	1963	1526.5	1972	1135.4
1955	1826.2	1964	1452.5	1973	1104.6
1956	1853.1	1965	1405.4	1974	1086.5
1957	1850.3	1966	1337.6	1975	1060.0
1958	1874.3	1967	1313.7	1976	1070.4
1959	1858.8	1968	1248.1	1978	1052.3
1960	1831.8	1969	1130.1	1979	1068.1
1961	1736.0	1970	1163.8		
1962	1629.5	1971	1137.0		
Year of birth	CTFR < 27	Year of birth	CTFR < 27	Year of birth	CTFR < 27
1950	1462.4	1964	1264.9	1974	639.2
1955	1526.9	1965	1184.7	1975	612.0
1956	1522.7	1966	1075.2	1976	599.1
1957	1549.0	1967	1002.5	1977	585.7
1958	1573.8	1968	900.1	1978	592.7
1959	1572.3	1969	843.8	1979	589.0
1960	1558.9	1970	773.7	1980	587.9
1961	1506.8	1971	728.0	1981	593.8
1962	1434.8	1972	703.6	1982	581.2
1963	1356.6	1973	678.2	1983	592.5

CTFR completed fertility up to the age of 45, 32, 27 years, accounted up to the year 2010

higher than the total fertility with 1394.2 born children per 1000 women of the named age in West Germany (Statistisches Bundesamt 2001; Staatliche Zentralverwaltung für Rechnungsführung und Statistik der DDR (1); Thüringer Landesamt für Statistik (1)).

Fifth Thesis Cohort fertility reacts with changing economic and social conditions and declines in the long run (independently from socialism or capitalism).

Cohort fertility of Thuringian women has declined in continuity since the cohort of 1959 born women (Table 4 and Fig. 1). This shows that the policy of population development of the GDR has not been successful. The cohort fertility sank over the cohorts and seems to reach the level of West German cohorts since the decade 1970, perhaps a little higher than that level.

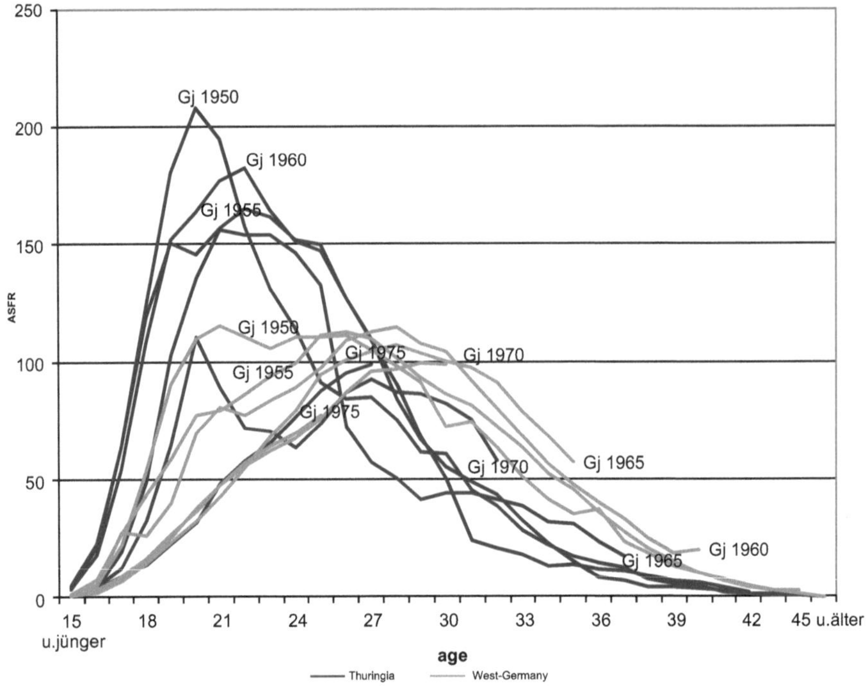

Fig. 1 Cohort fertility by age-specific fertility rate of mothers born in the years 1950, 1955, 1960, 1965, 1970, and 1975 in West Germany and Thuringia. (Source of data: Federal statistical office of Germany, Central state administration of bookkeeping and statistics of the GDR, Thuringian State Statistical Office: Statistical yearbooks of several years, own calculation)

Sixth Thesis The modus of the age of mothers when they give birth rises with life expectancy and leads to reduced fertility (timing-effect). This cuts cohort fertility.

The modus of the age of mothers when they give birth to their children was 21/22 years over a long period in Thuringia. This age was experienced by women up to the cohort born until 1970. The women cohort of the year of birth 1971 and later changed their behavior abruptly and raised their age to give birth to their children to the age of 26–28 (Table 5). West German women practiced this fertility pattern since the cohort 1960. This means that the Thuringian women have made a break in bearing children (Geburtenstreik) of 5–7 years (postponement). This explains the apparent rapid decline of the periodic total fertility rate to 772.5 born children per 1000 women at the age of 15–45 years in the first part of the 1990 decade up to 1994.

Seventh Thesis Important consequences of increasing lifespan and decreasing cohort fertility connote that population emerges not only demographically older (graying) but also that population develops demographically "greening." Both change population size and structure as well as cohort fertility in the long run.

The proportion of people 65 years and older increases from the year 1990 with 13.7–23.7 % in the year 2020 under the assumptions of the 12th coordinated population forecast of the Federal Statistical Office of Germany and the Thuringian

Table 5 Modus of the age of mothers when giving birth to their children for the cohorts of mothers born 1950, 1955–1981. (Source of data: Thuringian State Statistical Office: Statistical yearbooks, own calculation)

Year of birth	Modus	Year of birth	Modus	Year of birth	Modus
1950	20	1964	23	1974	28
1955	22	1965	21	1975	28
1956	22	1966	22	1976	28
1957	23	1967	21	1977	29
1958	21	1968	22	1978	29
1959	21	1969	21	1979	30
1960	22	1970	20	1980	{28}
1961	21	1971	26	1981	{29}
1962	22	1972	28		
1963	21	1973	27		

State Statistical Office (Thuringian State Statistical Office (1)). The proportion of people 20 years and younger will sink from 25.3 % in the year 1990 to 17.5 % in the year 2020 under the named assumptions (Table 6).

Scientific and public discussions focus first exclusively on the phenomenon of growing demographically older (e.g., Schimany 2003; Schirrmacher 2004; Thüringer Allgemeine 2004). In the recent past, demographic change in sense of necessary public measures took center stage. Dated back policy of the Federal Government of Germany and the Government of the Free State of Thuringia mainly responds to actual and forecasted demographic data and adjusts social systems and reduces benefits for families in part, because money lacks in public households. The other development, the demographically "under greening," took place already since the decade of 1980. Policy did not recognize this phenomenon or, if it should have recognized it, has had no means to establish measures to soften that development or to change its direction. A sustainable policy makes it necessary to identify actions, because a population grows from the bottom. A demographically "under green population" has no future. The newest developments in federal and state family policies in Germany and Thuringia let one hope for exceeding financial and handy support of families.

Table 6 Proportion of population of selected age groups in Thuringia from 1980 to 2020. (Source of data: Thuringian State Statistical Office: Statistical yearbooks, own calculation)

Year	Proportion of population in age of		
	Under 20	20–64	65 and older
	%		
1980	28.2	56.5	15.3
1990	25.3	60.9	13.7
2000	19.9	63.2	16.7
2010	12.5	64.4	23.0
2020	17.5	58.8	23.7

2.2 Variables of Partnership

In the following, different facts of partnership will be examined. At first, we deal with variables that are directly combined with the family. A decision for marriage and family with children locks out many economic choices, for example prosperity, material goods, traveling, visits of theaters, and so on.

Eighth Thesis Nuptiality rate fluctuates down by trend, the number of less binding civil unions rises. Meaning of matrimony as variable of fertility downsizes and reduces cohort fertility.

The nuptiality rate declines in Thuringia since 1980 with 8.5 marriages per 1000 inhabitants to 4.5 marriages per 1000 inhabitants in the year 2010. The sharpest cut took place in the year 1992 with 3.0 marriages per 1000 inhabitants. Up to now the nuptiality rate increases slightly and stands at half of the nuptiality rate in 1980 (Table 7). Today, nuptiality rate of Thuringia has adjusted and is similar to the nuptiality rate in Germany as a whole (Federal Statistical Office of Germany (1); Thuringian State Statistical Office (1)). Lower numbers of marriages are referred periodically to some extent to rising age of marriage (see ninth thesis).

Declining nuptial rate must be seen in connection with modern forms of civil union:

> 'The number of unmarried civil unions increased in the decade of 1980 also in the GDR, opposite to the number of singles. …Civil unions anticipated not only the marriage, but in many cases it had the function of realising the family life out of marriage.' (Huinink 1995, pp. 226/227) …. 'In East-Germany the civil unions in an own household is a phenomenon which worth mentioning occurs during the decade of 1980s' (Huinink 1995, p. 229).

The number of civil unions rose in both, the areas of West Germany and East Germany, in the recent quarter century. Their number increased in Germany from 1.6 million in 1994 to 2.6 million in 2009 about 60 %. At the same time, the number of civil unions without children as well as the number of civil unions with children increased (Federal Statistical Office of Germany (1)). The figures point

Table 7 Marriage and divorce in Thuringia in selected years since 1980. (Source: Thuringian State Statistical Office: Statistical yearbooks)

Year	Marriages	Divorces
	Per 1000 inhabitants	
1980	8.5	2.6
1989	7.6	2.9
1990	6.0	2.0
1991	3.2	0.6
1992	3.0	0.9
1995	3.5	1.4
2000	3.7	2.0
2002	3.6	2.0
2005	4.2	2.1
2010	4.5	1.8

Table 8 Civil unions in Thuringia 1994–2010. (Source: Thuringian State Statistical Office: Statistical yearbooks)

	Civil unions		
Jahr	Total	Childless	With children
	1000	%	
1994	51	45	55
1995	56	48	52
1996	59	49	51
1997	63	49	51
1998	63	52	48
1999	66	53	47
2000	71	51	49
2001	71	49	51
2002	72	50	50
2003	73	48	52
2004	80	48	52
2005	78	47	53
2006	73	56	43
2007	79	42	57
2008	87	57	43
2009	94	53	47
2010	97	58	42

out that civil unions are in the most cases childless in Germany. The situation in Thuringia had been different from that in Germany as a whole. The number of civil unions amounts to 97,000 in Thuringia in 2010 and has risen since 1994 about 90 % (Table 8). In Thuringia, more civil unions existed with children than childless up to the year 2005/2007. The rate turned since that time to behavior in West Germany and there are more civil unions childless nowadays.

Ninth Thesis Average age of marriage of single women and single men increases with life expectance. This reduces fertility and cuts cohort fertility.

The average age of marriage of single women increased in Thuringia from 23.3 years old in 1990 to 29.9 years old in the year 2010, the average age of marriage of single men from 25.5–33 years in the named time frame (Thuringian State Statistical Office (1)). From these empirical data we can draw the deduction that civil unions in Germany as a whole are frequently the consequence of the decision of two persons to live together without children. Special empirical tests on reasons to decide to marry or to live together in civil unions in combination to have children together are not known. Interviews on the desired number of children are not valid enough in this context. Discussions with our students let assume that one important reason is not to know whether you can live together with the married partner for the rest of your life and, if not, the costs of divorce are very high (compared with insignificant costs of divorce in the GDR).

In view of figures of age of marriage shows, that the tendency was also in the GDR to marry at later ages (Huinink 1995, p. 222). Empirical studies come to the result that 20 % of persons of the cohort born in 1959/1961 have married during occupational training; the proportion was 60 % with graduates of universities (Huinink 1995, p. 250). Huinink found out on the basis of empirical cohort data, that

> the age, when founding the first own household, didn't increase again in the GDR in the decade of 1980. …While it stayed relatively unchanged for men in our cohorts, it decreased clearly for women particularly comparing the years of birth 1929-31 with younger cohorts. …The contrast between the increased age of marriage and the declined average age, when founding an own household, reflects the increased pattern of life for young men as well as women to be independent of the home of their parents (Huinink 1995, p. 224/225).

This behavior, which developed during the socialist system in Thuringia, grew stronger in the decade of 1990 under the conditions of market economy. Civil union as a form of life increased percentage wise, so did the age of marriage. This means that young people put more emphasis on completing their occupational training and university degrees and—so we can assume because of the high rate of unemployment of young people—find a job before they marry.

Tenth thesis The non-legitimate fertility rate increases and does not compensate for the loss of legitimate fertility.

As a next step, the percentage of children born out of wedlock will be analyzed. When we look at the children born out of wedlock since transition 1989/1990 we see, that the non-legitimate fertility rate was reduced for a short time in Thuringia from 405.2 per 1000 births of surviving children in the year 1991 to 326.5 in the year 1994. Ever since, the non-legitimate fertility rate increased up to 596.7 per 1000 live births in the year 2010 (Thuringian State Statistical Office (1)). Today more than half of the live births are non-legitimate births in Thuringia. The non-legitimate fertility rate of Thuringia indeed is one of the lowest in the new federal states in Germany after the transition of 1989/1990, but on the other hand it is nearly twice as high as the non-legitimate fertility rate for Germany as a whole (Federal Statistical Office of Germany (1)).

> 'In the former GDR, the proportion of births, that happened at least two years before marriage, continuously increased …' (Huinink 1995, pp. 235/236).
> 'The survivor function … shows, that three quarter of women in West-Germany, which have born their first child in the decade of 1990, have married before their child was born. In East-Germany this proportion is much less than a half … the half of West-German women had been married already at the time of conception … We find other patterns in East-Germany. Less than one quarter of women had been married at time of their conception and the survivor function is also more flat in the months before and after birth than in West-Germany' (Huinink and Konietzka 2003, p. 80)

This means that marriage got less importance in the last years and civil union got more importance in Germany now. Marriage gets less importance to explain fertility rates as a whole than in former times. Unfortunately, there are no official data on fertility in civil unions available.

Eleventh Thesis As consequence of decreasing nuptiality rate (eighth thesis), the divorce rate is relatively stable. Divorce influences periodic fertility to a slight extent.

The divorce rate per 1000 inhabitants in Thuringia increased from 2.6 in the year 1980 to 2.9 in the year 1989, decreased to 2.0 in 1990 and 0.6 in 1991, respectively to 0.9 in 1992. The main reason can be seen in the establishment of the rule of law including family law, which took time until courts became workable. Furthermore

> ...the attitudes of Thuringian women are clearly that economic reasons made them continue their marriage despite of crises in their connection with their husbands (Gensicke 1998, p. 131).

In the following years the divorce rate increased to 1.8 per 1000 inhabitants and remained around this level for several years (Table 7). The figure is a third less than in the years of transition 1989/1990 and approximates today divorce rate for Germany as a whole.

The lower level of divorce since transition 1989/1990 also has to be seen in front of the background of fewer marriages during that time.

Twelfth Thesis Abortions are expression of life planning of women and reduce the periodic and cohort fertility.

A further important variable in connection with fertility is the level of abortions in a country. The number of abortions in Thuringia sank from the long run high level in the GDR (highest figure in preceding districts of Thuringia in the year 1973 with 30.9 legal abortions per 1000 women at the age between 15 and 45 years old) until the years of transition 1989/1990 more than a half and fluctuates around 10 legal abortions per 1000 women since 1997. The total number of legal abortions fluctuates in the last years slightly less than 4000–5000 per annum with around 17,000 live births per annum (Thuringian State Statistical Office (1)). Thuringia lost more than 80,000 babies in the 1990th decade and further more than 40,000 babies in the first decade of twenty-first century. Thuringia abortions are in the top group of federal states in Germany; only the states of Saxony-Anhalt, Mecklenburg-West Pomerania and the three federal city states Berlin, Hamburg, and Bremen show higher level (Federal Statistical Office of Germany(1)). Nowadays onethird of legal abortions are performed in Thuringia by women at the age under 25 years old. More than 40 % are executed by women older than 30 years; in principle, children of second and higher parity[1] are aborted (Thuringian State Statistical Office (1)).

Summary of Facts of Partnership In conclusion, analysis of facts of partnership shows that the disposition for marriage in Thuringia sank since the transition 1989/1990 and the disposition for civil union increased since then. Parallel with this development the legitimate fertility sank and the non-legitimate fertility rose. Experiences with socialism and experiences with capitalism in connection with less religion in the new federal states compared with West German federal states led to

[1] Ranking of a child by birth.

a halt of bearing children in the first half of the decade 1990. Young people, after leaving their parents, more and more live first in civil unions. They marry when they have finished their occupational training and their university degrees and when they have found a job. The divorce rate is now less than at the time of the end of socialism. The influence of legal abortions on fertility sank over time and fluctuates on a lower level nowadays than before.

2.3 *Economic Variables*

In the following, important economic variables will be analyzed that have—in sense of family economics—strong influence on fertility. Transition from socialism to capitalism is characterized among other things by changing the economic system from public property to private property. The latter does not work under governmental plans as in socialism but under the conditions of a free (social) market economy. So it was clear that the transition 1989/1990 would lead to a completely changed and now free economy in Thuringia. People had to alter and to adjust their economic behavior inter alia. There was no longer a shortage of certain goods, but from one day to the other one could select among a large variety of goods and buy them, if one had the money to pay for these. This meant that the experiences of 40 years of scarcity had hardly any meaning any more, and the people had to learn the ropes in a market economy starting from their socialist backgrounds. This situation was unique and combined with much anticipation. At that time, it was already clear that the different expectations could not be fulfilled completely by politicians, economy, and welfare state. The question in connection with our investigation is in which way and to what extent lag between anticipation and real situation and resulting disappointment influenced fertility behavior in Thuringia.

Thirteenth thesis Changing economic structure strengthening the tertiary sector reduces periodic and cohort fertility.

The economic structure of Thuringia has changed strongly since 1989. In the first years of this space of time, the secondary sector had the biggest importance just as during socialist times of the GDR. The share of secondary sector went down rapidly and since 2002 it is nearly identical with the proportion in West Germany. The tertiary sector dominated relative quickly, for example in the year 1996, it had a proportion of 59.8 % of employees and this was only slightly under the proportion in West Germany. The sharp decline of the secondary sector and the steep increase of the tertiary sector show the speed of the transition process. Today, economic structures in Thuringia and in West Germany are nearly the same, though we must assess that the increase of tertiary sector at the expense of secondary sector occurred on a slightly smaller scale than in Western Germany since 2002 (Table 9).

Fourteenth Thesis Strengthening tertiary sector improves opportunities for female employment, raises opportunity costs and reduces periodic and cohort fertility.

The proportion of female employees is clearly lower in the secondary sector than the share of male employees in this sector. On the other hand, the proportion of female employees in the tertiary sector is clearly higher (Thuringian State Statistical

Table 9 Economic structure in Thuringia and West Germany measured on the proportion of employees between 1990 and 2009[a]). (Source: Federal statistical office of Germany; State Statistical Office of Thuringia in foundation)

	West Germany				Thuringia				
Sectors	1990	1996	2002	2009	1989	1990	1996	2002	2009
	%								
Primary	3.7	2.8	2.4	1.6	10.1	7.5	3.6	3.1	2.6
Secondary	40.6	35.2	32.5	29.4	54.5	51.0	36.6	32.7	29.1
Tertiary	55.8	62.1	65.1	69.0	35.4	41.5	59.8	64.2	68.2

[a] Results of German Mikrozensus and employment statistic of new federal states

Office (1)). Table 10 shows first the increase of gainful employment of both gender and second that the participation of women as a proportion of economic active persons in all age groups is lower than the share of men in 2001. However the gap decreased to this day, and in the age of 40–45 the share of economic participation of men and women is equal, in age inside 45–50 the economic participation of women is higher than participation of men. Opportunity costs of fertility rose.

Fifteenth Thesis Relatively lower net income compared with other neighboring territories reduces periodic fertility and cohort fertility in the long run.

East–West relationship of payments and salaries depend with a certain fluctuation on the branch of economic activity. Till this day, average salary amounts to about 70–80% since 1991 though the gap decreased slightly in recent years (Federal Statistical Office of Germany 1).

Table 10 Proportion of economic active persons in Thuringia 2001 and 2010 by age groups and sex[a]. (Source: Thuringian State Staistical Office: Statistical Yearbooks 2002 and 2011—Results of German Mikrozensus—own calculation)

Age from to under years	Labor force 2001[b]			Labor force 2010[c]		
	Men	Women	Total	Men	Women	Total
	%					
15–20	39.2	24.9	32.3	32.6	31.3	30.0
20–25	68.8	59.7	64.5	65.4	57.6	62.6
25–30	80.9	68.3	75.5	79.5	73.0	76.5
30–35	84.9	74.5	79.6	88.2	78.7	83.7
35–40	85.7	79.0	82.5	88.4	83.9	85.6
40–45	84.7	78.7	81.7	86.6	86.6	88.2
45–50	84.4	79.1	81.9	84.7	85.6	84.6
50–55	81.9	71.6	76.8	84.2	78.7	81.5
55–60	60.4	49.3	54.8	75.9	69.2	72.5
65 and above	6.7	1.6	3.8	3.7	1.7	2.5
15–65	69.0	58.6	63.9	75.8	71.0	73.1

[a] Calculated as proportion of relevant age group
[b] 2001: population April
[c] 2010: annual average population

> 'On regard to the level of wages and salaries, we can find out, that the structure of employment in Thuringia reference to gender of employees let assume higher level of wages and salaries in West-Germany. …Regarding to differences in wages and salaries between men and women but also between industrial sector and service trades as a whole just as within the single lines of business and furthermore between single firms of the same line we found out: main reasons are deviations of the structure of qualification and occupation, such as training, kind of job, age of life, duration of occupation et cetera' (Uth 2000, p. 28). 'The structure of employees and its development on regard to gender are certain obstacles for a higher level and a better development of wages and salaries of Thuringian employees' (Uth 2000, p. 30).

The proportion of salaries of female employees compared with male employees is higher in Thuringia and the other new federal states than in West Germany.

> This results particularly from higher qualification of women in the new federal states … and a higher proportion of women which have jobs with more responsibility (Uth 2000, p. 29).

Sixteenth Thesis Changed family structure with more single parents tends to result in less income and reduces periodic and cohort fertility.

The context we deal with, an evaluation of the economic situation makes it necessary to look at the incomes of private households and families. Unemployment rate stood at 15–19 % since 1992 (Table 12) and reduces since 2006. Unemployment damped down the budget of families and single parents over a period of 15 years. The effect is explicitly lesser since 2006. Net income situation of couples living together, married, or in civil union has clearly improved over the period since 1991. On the contrary, net income situation of single parents has also improved, but obviously less than that of couples, also when taken into desideration that the necessary income for single educators is less than for couples. The relative situation of net incomes of single parents by contrast with couples got worse over time (Table 11).

Marriage and family stood under protection of the constitution both in the Federal Republic of Germany and in the GDR.

> 'The importance of family was legally written down in the GDR with the legislation on family of the year 1966 and population policy as well as women's politics were fitted out equally to this importance. The conjugal and living together in the family was favoured and sponsored under both aims the support of bearing children and simultaneous realization of economic activity and being mother of children' (Rheinbay-Lehmann 1998, p. 275).
> 'The social changes during the process of German unification have changed the functions of family and household as well as the position of women within family and partnership. …Particularly the increase of tasks within the family refers to women at first. … It makes it more difficult for women within the family so that the relationships within the families got more difficult because of economic difficulties since transition' (Rheinbay-Lehmann 1998, p. 277).

We can summarize, that households of single parents and households with one or more unemployed persons have seen their financial situation worsen since 1989/1990.

Seventeenth Thesis Net-income of private households and families increases opportunity costs and influences differently the fertility of couples and singles.

Table 11 Unmarried children living in families in Thuringia combined with monthly net income of the family in 1991, 2002, and 2010 (percentage). Thuringian State Statistical Office: Statistical Report: Selected topics of development in Thuringia 1991–2002 and Statistical Year-books–Results of German Mikrocensus; partial own estimation

Year	Under 1300	1300–2000	2000 and more
	%		
Total			
1991	56.7	31.7	10.5
2002	18.1	24.9	51.9
2010	1.3	22.8	63.7
Couples			
1991	50.1	33.1	6.9
2002	11.3	23.7	64.8
2010	4.1	14.9	80.9
Single parents			
1991	84.3	[4.7]	[]
2002	50.5	28.2	15.9
2010	39.4	46.4	14.3

Families without income as well as self-employed in agriculture, fisheries, and family worker are not included. Own calculation—data partly evaluated
[ ] result not representative

The employment rate was around 81 % in Thuringia at the beginning of the transition of 1989/1990 and many more women worked and earned money than nowadays. Compared with the situation of the GDR now in the market economy, men and women have fewer chances to work and to earn income. This does not mean that net income including social benefits measured in purchasing power is lower now than before, but it is perceived as lower.

> 'The hope of many East-German women did not get fulfilled in various cases: to continue as before their ideas of life and occupation under the conditions of a free social and political system. Also their hope was an illusion to transfer some elements of socialist society into the new free system. The West-German model was transferred nearly one to one. That means also that achievements were not transferred to the united Germany which have been seen positively from West-German women as women policy' (Rosenzweig 2002, p. 193). 'One central result referring to the field of "work" is the finding that economic activity of East-German women is of highest importance for them feeling well and for their ego. This ego has been considerably affected at Thuringian women during time which was investigated' (1991 to 1993) (Rheinbay-Lehmann 1998, p. 201). 'Simultaneously it can be said that women in the GDR did not work mainly because of equal rights though this was officially said very often' (Rheinbay-Lehmann 1998, p. 202). 'Economic activity fulfils for women on the one side the financial necessity of living, on the other side an urgent function for their ego' (Rheinbay-Lehmann 1998, p. 149).

Eighteenth Thesis Increasing share of costs per children raises opportunity costs and reduces periodic and cohort fertility.

Including the costs assuring that parents share equally in the time devoted to child raising, the cost for two children amount to between 233,000 and 251,000 €

for parents with academic degrees and between 182,000 and 197,000 € for parents with professional degrees.

> The costs to support and to take care of two children up to their 17th year amount to about 200,000 EURO. There arise further opportunity costs between 15,000 and 18,000 EURO for couples, which give up equally their economic activity (Hufnagel 2002, p. 114).

These empirical values amount to average calculated costs per children of monthly 500 €. The average costs in Thuringia are surely somewhat lower, since the costs of living are slightly lower than in West Germany. Therefore, and because the level of net income is only around 70–80 % (see fifteenth thesis) the costs of educating a child are relatively higher in Thuringia than in West Germany. The opportunity costs are not yet taken into account. That means that couples with only one child must give up a relatively high proportion of their consumption during the time of educating their children. This part goes beyond securing the children's livelihood. The burden is higher when opportunity costs are included.

> When you have little children and if mother and father want to share equally their economic activity, they must do it during this phase without consumption that goes over the fundamental needs, for example: vacation, car, to go out, a demanding hobby, et cetera (Hufnagel 2002, p. 124).

Nineteenth Thesis Increase of consumer price index leads to shifts in the consumption function and reduces periodic and cohort fertility.

In Thuringia the annual consumer price index dramatically rose at the beginning of the 1990s to 11.2, 10.1, and 4 %; the perceived inflation was clearly higher. During that time, the birth rate and the fertility rates sank dramatically. An important reason for this periodic decrease is the intermission of young women formerly bearing children at the beginning of their 20s. Since the year 1995, the consumer price index sank to around 2 %, sank under 2 % since 1999, escalated to more than 2 % before banking crisis 2008 and sank articulately under 1 % since that time (Federal Statistical Office of Germany (1)). Since 1995, total fertility rate rose again to 1.4 children per 15–45 years old women in 2010 (Fig. 2). The main reason for this is that women at the age around their mid-20s started to bear children again. The data show the connection and consequently the dependency on fertility and economic, especially financial, variables.

Proportion of expenditures in the budget of private households has changed as compared with the situation in the GDR. Technical goods for daily life have become cheaper since transition. Food, clothes, and furniture are more expensive now. On the other hand, rent, energy, preschools, hotels, and luxury goods are much more expensive now. The development of the consumer price index of all private households is negatively correlated with total fertility rate.

Twentieth Thesis Unemployment reduces net income of private households and singles, leads to postponement of desired children and reduces periodic fertility for a time; long-term unemployment could boost cohort fertility.

Unemployment is a further important variable, because unemployment reduces the net income of a single person and of the household as an economic unity. Reduction of unemployment benefits leads to smaller net income of certain groups

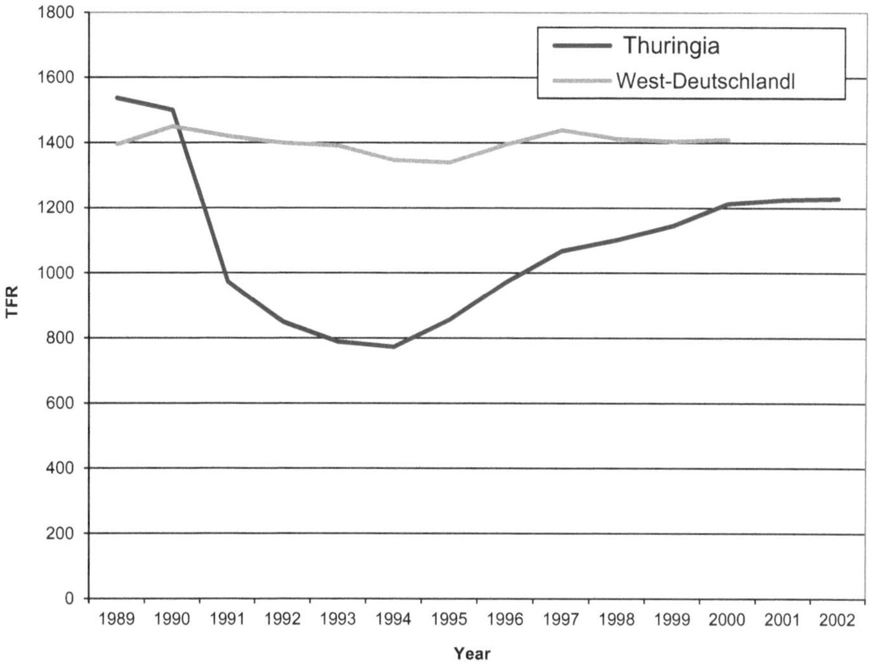

Fig. 2 Development of the periodic total fertility rate in Thuringia and West Germany from 1989 to 2002. (Source of data: Federal Statistical Office of Germany, Thuringian State Statistical Office: Statistical Yearbooks)

of the population. For countries in transition, this must be seen under the changed conditions from a socialist to a market economy. In the GDR unemployment did not exist officially. This was defined in article 15 of the constitution of the GDR. There was a large share of hidden unemployment, but a description and explanation of this phenomenon goes beyond the scope of this paper.

As said before, the proportion of employed persons to the population at the age of 15–65 years amounted to 81 % in Thuringia in the year 1989. It decreased to 72.2 % in 1991 and sank all in all furthermore to around 70 % nowadays. Employment rate of men measured to the population at the age between 15 and 65 years was 67.3 % in 2002 and 74.3 % in 2010, that one of women 58.9 % respectively 69.1 % (Thuringian State Statistical Office (1)). The gap between men and women downsized in favor of women.

The development of the unemployment rates shows that there are more women unemployed than men, though the lag between both rates got smaller in the last years (Table 12). This corresponds to the development of the gender-specific employment rates. The dramatic increase of the unemployment rate correlates negatively to the dramatic decrease of the periodic total fertility rate up to the year 1994; the reason is that women at the beginning of their 20s pause to bear children. The following decrease of the unemployment rate correlates negatively to the

Table 12 Unemployment rate as annual average in Thuringia 1991—2010. (Source of data: Source of data: Thüringer Landesamt für Statistik: Statistical yearbooks—Change of method since 2003 related to all civilian labor force)

Year	Unemployment rate		
	Total	Men	Women
1991	10.2	7.6	12.8
1992	15.4	10.1	21.0
1993	16.3	10.8	22.7
1994	16.5	10.8	22.6
1995	15.0	10.5	19.8
1996	16.7	13.6	20.0
1997	19.1	15.9	22.5
1998	18.3	15.8	21.0
1999	16.5	14.2	18.9
2000	16.5	14.7	18.4
2001	16.5	15.2	17.8
2002	17.2	16.5	17.9
2003	16.7	15.9	17.8
2004	16.7	16.0	17.7
2005	17.1	16.5	17.9
2006	15.6	14.5	16.9
2007	13.1	11.7	17.7
2008	11.2	10.2	12.4
2009	11.4	11.2	11.5
2010	9.8	9.9	9.8

increase of the total fertility rate (Fig. 2). Women started again to bear children in the mid of their 20s.

Twenty-First Thesis Mainly young women emigrate from a territory that is not estimated to support their life planning. This reduces periodic fertility.

The extent of illegal emigration (alignment) was one of the main reasons that led to the transition 1989/1990. Since then, especially young women emigrated from Thuringia predominantly to West Germany.

> 'Emigration is mainly influenced by individual aims like to secure living, perspectives to realize personal needs and needs of the family by economic activity' (Bartz and Jahn 1996, p. 189). 'Particularly young Thuringian women have a fundamental positive attitude towards family, but they restrict that they want to shift the foundation of their family to a later moment at least when they have secured their professional situation' (Rheinbay-Lehmann 1998, p. 368).

Lack of chances for occupational training and high unemployment respond especially young women to look for alternatives. They find these alternatives in federal states of West Germany and foreign countries that show a better economic development than they see daily in Thuringia. The dramatic increase of emigration from Thuringia to West Germany shortly before and in the first years after the transition 1989/1990 was answered by the young women with a pause in bearing children.

Since 1995, the number of emigrations oscillated around 40,000 for many years, since turn of century down on tendency. The fertility is continued with a time lag. Thuringian women persist often and bear their children in the state they immigrated.

Twenty-Second Thesis Good (financial) chances for children to grow up worsen for reasons like, for example, perceived bad perspectives of the future, unemployment depending on social benefits, etc. This reduces periodic and cohort fertility.

The number of married couples without children rose 44 % by the year 2010 since 1991 with an increasing tendency over time. On the other hand, the number of married couples with children sank 49 % by the year 2010. The number of single parents rose 8.3 % to 121,000 by 2002 with a decreasing tendency since then to 85,000 by 2010 (Thuringian State Statistical Office (1)). The proportion of unmarried children living together with a married couple (in most cases parents and step parents) sank from 77 % in the year 1991 to 70 % in 2010. During the same time, the share of children living together with a single educating parent rose from 23 % in 1991 to 30 % in the year 2010[2].

Together with by trend increasing proportion of children living in civil union, there develops a change of circumstances in which children grow up. In conclusion: to give children a good chance to grow up becomes more difficult in a market economy than under socialism; this leads especially in the phase of transition to a pause in bearing children.

Summary of Results with Economic Variables Changing economic structures, exceptionally in transition processes, lead to high unemployment. Women are more affected by unemployment than men. The net income situation of couples with children and single parents improved since 1991, though wages and salaries in Thuringia are the lowest of the German states in the whole time till this day and 20–30 % less than in West Germany. The situation is perceived as deterioration, though it has improved. At the same time, the proportions of expenditures in the budget of people have changed in comparison with the time before under socialism. Food and clothes are more expensive, rent and pre-schools are much more expensive now. The perspectives of the future are seen negatively, young people, especially young women emigrate to states of West Germany and others are disappointed and discouraged. The costs of children increased and the opportunity costs rose as well.

2.4 *Sociological Variables*

The GDR was in a leading position compared with other socialist countries referring to luxury goods (Gensicke 1996, p. 116). In consequence of transition in 1989/1990, it was immediately possible for the citizens to buy luxury goods in much better

[2] By reasons of changed statistical definition of Families, above named specifications for 2010 are own appraisals on the basis of Table 14.

quality than during socialism. People had saved enough money, because costs of living were low and luxury goods were expensive and you had to wait for a long time until you got the good you wanted. For example, you had to wait for 10 years after ordering the small "plastic car" Trabi, 18 years for a better car "Wartburg". From one day to the other it was possible to buy luxury goods in better quality and without waiting for a long time.

Twenty-Third Thesis A lot of catching up technical equipment leads to shifts in the consumption function and reduces periodic fertility. If fulfilling the needs takes a long time, cohort fertility will be reduced.

It is not surprising that the population tries to seize upon better goods of luxury. In the Thuringian case at the beginning of the 1990th decade, travelling, sale of west cars, and similar objects boomed. The stock of automobiles rose from 751,473 cars in 1992 to 1,228,181 cars at 2000 about 63 %; it sank to 1,157,305 in 2011 in consequence of financial crisis (Thuringian State Statistical Office (1)). Considerable parts are private cars. But also precaution for the future took place, for example life insurances, savings accounts for building houses, etc. At the same time, the degree of equipment in private households with further technical equipment increased and partly even went over the level in West Germany (Table 13).

The increased expenditures for durable goods and precautionary savings, insurance, etc. for the future correlates negatively with the fertility rates, i.e. periodic fertility declined with increased expenditures, because bearing children was halted. Periodic fertility rose again, when saturation and clear approach to the West German level had been reached. People have more money for children at their disposal since the expenditures for these goods went down. The consumption function changed again. Women in their 20s began to bear children again and their fertility rose.

Twenty-Fourth Thesis For modern women nowadays, giving birth is in competition with self-determined life and financial independence. This breeds to increasing opportunity costs and reduces periodic and cohort fertility.

Table 13 Level of technical equipment in private households in Thuringia and West Germany 1993, 1998, 2003, and 2008. (Source: Thuringian State Statistical Office: Statistical yearbooks 2005 and 2011)

	Thuringia				West Germany	
Type	1993	1998	2003	2008	2003	2008
	%					
Car	66.6	71.9	76.2	76.2	78.0	77.9
TV	95.5	97.9	95.8	95.5	94.2	93.9
Videocamera/camcorder	5.9	16.1	24.2	24.2	22.0	19.3
Personal computer	14.1	36.4	59.5	72.4	62.4	76.3
Refrigarator	90.4	99.4	99.1	98.3	98.7	98.6
Dishwasher	2.6	24.7	47.2	54.7	59.0	64.2
Microwave	13.0	41.2	64.1	71.9	63.2	69.5
Dryer	3.0	16.4	25.7	29.8	40.4	42.3

The number of second and more children of married couples sank 37% since 1991, while the number of second children of single parents rose 7.3% until 2002 and sank 62% until 2010. The number of first children of married couples sank 35% and the number of first children of single parents decreased 10%; altogether, the number of first children sank 18% (Thuringian State Statistical Office (1), Table 14). That means that the number of childless couples rises (decreasing number of first children) and the number of couples with two and more children decrease. We assess tendency to one child partnership.

> Economic activities of women follow different patterns in East-Germany and West-Germany…. East-German women have a barrier up to now to adopt the traditional western model of family of a fulltime working man and a part-time working woman. …Women protest against the difficulties and argue to have the right to decide for family and job at the same time (Rosenzweig 2002, pp. 187)

Today, it is often difficult for families and civil unions to decide pro children and it is still more difficult to opt for second or third children.

> Contrary to the times of the GDR, women feel a large insecurity in the fields of labor market and family since the unification (Rheinbay-Lehmann 1998, p. 363).

Table 14 Kind of families' and number of children in Thuringia 1991—2010. (Source: Thuringian State Statistical Office: Statistical report: Selected topics of development in Thuringia 1991—2002—Results of German Mikrozensus; Statisical Report: Haushold and family in Thuringia 2010—results of Mikrozensus)

Years	Families[a]					
	Without unmarried children			With unmarried children		
	Total	Children	Together	One children	Two children	Three and more
	1000					
	Total					
1991	1023.6	528.8	494.6	263.0	195.0	36.6
2002	980.6	573.9	406.7	236.5	142.4	27.9
2010	1038	759	279[b]	183	89	16
	Married couples					
1991	656.8	273.8	382.9	182.3	169.0	31.6
2002	574.8	289.2	285.6	149.1	114.4	22.1
2010	507	312[c]	195[d]	118	64	14
	Solitary persons/single parents					
1991	366.8	254.9	111.8	80.7	26.0	[]
2002	405.8	284.7	121.1	87.4	27.9	[]
2010	531	447	84	65	16	[]

[a] Over time, definition of Families has been modified in federal statistics: today family includes married couples, civil unions and same-sex unions
[b] Including civil unions and same-sex unions: 325
[c] Including civil unions and same-sex unions: 364
[d] Including civil unions and same-sex unions: 241

Twenty-Fifth Thesis (Perceived) worsening public family benefits and advantages for mothers with children in working conditions lead to time shortening for mothers and reduce periodic and cohort fertility.

The transition in 1989/1990 from socialism to a market economy led to changes in the system of public family benefits. While parents had been familiar with perceived better situation in the GDR in their experience, the situation has changed and nearly from one day to the other became completely new for them. Now, they have to take personal care of their children to a larger extent than before under socialism.

> Up to the year 1989 public organisations have done the socialization of children. Since then this responsibility is transmitted to parents. New tasks for parents came up not only because of shut down of day-care centres and the stopped care of pupils but also because of new liberty in the education of children, selection of schools, choice of occupational training and so on. Furthermore, the care of old and sick people is not any more in the common responsibility of socialist society. This must be solved by single persons. Also material duties have increased within the family. In many cases lunch is cancelled in canteen and school, so that food must be prepared often at home. Those downstream duties mean frequently a further stress for women (Rheinbay-Lehmann 1998, p. 278).

Since the beginning of the year 1991, West German family policy is valid in Thuringia. For example, this refers to following changes:

> The possibilities of exemption to take care of sick children have been reduced dramatically since 1st of January 1991, the aid in case of birth of a child and interest-free loans for young couples have been stopped at 31st of December 1990. The holiday for mothers after birth of her children (Wochenurlaub) is reduced from twenty weeks to eight weeks since the beginning of 1991, the laws referring to maternity leave (Babyjahr) and assistance for mothers (Mutterunterstützung) are replaced by the federal laws of educational holiday (Erziehungsurlaub) and child-raising-benefits (Erziehungsgeld). The special dismissal protection (Kündigungsschutz) of single educating mothers and fathers existed only up to 31st of December 1991; the monthly workday for the household (Hausarbeitstag) has been abolished since the year 1992 (Rheinbay-Lehmann 1998, p. 282).

Twenty-Sixth Thesis The value of children has decreased; children have assumed a lower priority than other aims of self-determined life planning. This reduces periodic and cohort fertility.

Values have changed, children are clearly perceived as luxury goods. On the basis of the above-mentioned desires and the priority of first a job to earn money and then children, we find out, in conclusion, that it is necessary for people to spend much time to find and to secure a job. Hence, there is little opportunity to spend time together with a partner; the result is self-isolation and fewer children are born.

Twenty-Seventh Thesis Young women prefer a lexicographical utility function of reproduction behavior. Women with self-determined life planning and work-life—balance follow time sequences.

First Qualified school education and qualified professional training;

Second over period of professional training, young women live predominantly in civil union;

Third during and after concluded professional training life is conducted following the philosophy "for a start to experience somewhat, to acquire something, then family";

Fourth predominant difficult job hunting for equivalent educational attainment appropriate paid employment; partial, temporary acceptance of under-qualified job;

Fifth collateral security in consequence of indefinite employment;

Sixth validation of career;

Seventh giving birth.

Before Named, Preferred Time Sequences Reduce Periodic and Cohort Fertility: The Biological Clock Ticks

In representative samples the desire to have a family is very strong. Simultaneously, on the agenda of East German women there is strong desire to earn money.

> The proportion of women is very small which say "at first children than job" (7.1 % in 1991 and 3.9 % in 1992) as well as the proportion of women which did not wish to have a job and instead of this orientate fully on family. This possibility was desired by 6.2 % in 1990 and only 2.6 % in 1992 of interviewed women (Rheinbay-Lehmann 1998, p. 310).

In many cases marriage and giving birth are sought after in the following sequence:

> at first I want to experience somewhat, to acquire something and then have a family (Rheinbay-Lehmann 1998, p. 312).

Summary of Results from Other Social Variables Nowadays, women have clear high preferences for full-time employment. Though young women desire to have children it is a question of time giving birth. The time of professional training increased and the available time for children went down.

2.5 Overall Summary and Suggestion for Improvement

Above described research result confirms our basic thesis that economic and social conditions as well as citizens' behavior change over a long period and these alterations lead to changing reproduction behavior.

Basic outlooks on home life stand in the background of those priorities described above. These beliefs have developed in Thuringia during the times of the GDR and as a consequence of the transition 1989/1990 from socialist to capitalistic times. In the literature, this is discussed with different results. Some authors establish on the basis of empirical data a basic difference in outlook between East Germany and West Germany (Meulemann 1998), others establish on the basis of other empirical data that several ideas on human life have adjusted between East Germany and West Germany and are widely identical nowadays. Whatever, our analysis shows that there has happened a continuous decline of fertility over time, both in socialism and in capitalism. People respond to changes in the circumstances of their life regardless of political system. In Thuringia, a sharp and relatively quick change took place in connection with the transition of 1989/1990 that led to an alteration in the reproductive behavior of people born in the years before 1970, and there was a sharp change in the behavior of young people born since 1971.

> Realists are to find more in cohorts of younger people in the East of Germany (Gensicke 1996, p. 128).

The empirical findings described in this essay explain very well on the basis of the economics of the family why young women of the birth year 1971 and later paused in bearing children after transition for 5–7 years. Job and children are not compatible to that extent that women with self-determined life planning prefer. The younger generation adjusts to the changed situation and tries to find ways for self-determination and satisfaction in life, for example like emigration to the western part of Germany and adaptation of fertility timing. Periodic fertility assimilated in Thuringia in line with West Germany. Looking to cohort fertility we discover that fertility has decreased in Thuringia since the cohort of 1959 born women both, under socialism and capitalism.

It has been shown that at least 27 variables influence the reproduction of mankind. In described investigations, there could be corroborated only to a certain extent the basic assumption of the economics of the family considering opportunity costs when deciding giving birth. It is necessary to analyze and handle clearly more variables in mathematical family models than this is done actually. The single 27 variables described in this essay can be depicted partially in cardinal form, or only ordinal. On the one hand, there exist difficulties in the grade of ordinal variables, and on the other hand, there are difficulties in the unambiguous sequence of the characteristic features of ordinal variables. The dependences of the variables can be established only by empirical surveys on the basis of a near to complete fertility model; this needs much time to develop and establishing would be indeed expensive. Given budgetary constraints, the solution can hardly be to cut down on theory and with Ockham's razor, reduce the issue to one or at most two or three variables on readily available data. This yields only an insufficient basis for effective policy making and inefficient political activities as well as costs rise.

3 Wilhelm von Humboldt's Images Defining Political Principles of the State

Fundamentals of Humboldt's state liberalism will be condensed accounted below. 'Principle of public policy has to act on the assessment of individual person and his maximum ultimate purposes' (Humboldt 1991, p. 21). 'Every individual person is to be relished most disengaged liberty to emerge himself as his singularity … each individual person according to his desiderata and his affections only restricted to limits of his potencies and his authorizations' (Humboldt 1991, p. 28). 'Person concerns himself directly or indirectly with fulfilment physical desiderata or generally to achieve exterior objects' (Humboldt 1991, p. 35). 'Man aspires at liberty, woman at custom' (Humboldt 1991, p. 40). The state has to provide for exterior security in sense of protection in front of foreign enemies (Humboldt 1991, Chap. V) and internal security in sense of security for all citizens (Humboldt 1991, Chap. VI). Education of individual person is indispensable of the state and affords public impact on citizen's custom (Humboldt 1991, Chap. VI). 'The state has to abstain all of care for positive wealth of citizens and has to realize no more grade than necessary for securing against themself and against foreign enemies' (Humboldt 1991, p. 52). Positive wealth of a nation (today, it is named social security) is no duty of state. Internal security consist of legal rules concerning laws of police affairs (Humboldt 1991, Chap. X), laws of civil affairs (Humboldt 1991, Chap. XI), ordinary jurisdiction (Humboldt 1991, Chap. XII), penal jurisdiction (Humboldt 1991, Chap. XIII), guaranty relating to immaturity (Humboldt 1991, Chap. XIV) and financial means preserving general government (Humboldt 1991, Chap. XV).

Summarized, Humboldt restricts state liberalism on public imperative and strains duties of a state on essential challenges and well-defined tasks to guarantee external security, legal regulation, and liberty of citizens. Education exhibits focus of his state liberalism, because education offers people to comprehend complex circumstances and connections. The principles describe not a minimal state ore laissez-faire state, but it disregards economical inclusions of a welfare state. Humboldt's political principles of the state imply no public impact to take influence on population development and reproduction behavior. Modern welfare states imply additional wealth of complete society or social classes.

4 Résumé

Humboldt's political principles of the state have been the first attempt to arrange images defining materialities of public tasks as activity of public sector which is prescribed by law. It describes—based on precepts of John Locke—ideas of the beginning liberalism in Germany and reflects the spirit of the time. Humbolt's "pure" liberalism refuses social security as duty of the state. Aftermath, socio-liberalism has been emerged among others and postulates public aid money to back up politically desired public developments. On this account, above mentioned and other public family benefits and advantages for mothers with children in working are parts of family policy as well as demographic policy today.

Beside above described state liberalism, Humboldt designed humanistic education reform. With regard to universities, he required that 'public cultural bureaucracy should refrain as far as possible from research and science; government should only concede possibility of participation with respect to funding university and appointment of tenured professors' (Lutz-Bachmann 2011, p. 2).

References

Althammer, J. (2000). *Ökonomische Theorie der Familienpolitik*. Heidelberg: Physica-Verlag.

Bartz, B., & Jahn, G. (1996). Aspekte der beruflichen Eingliederung von Ausländern. In I. Graudenz (Hrsg.), *Forschungsfeld Aussiedler: Ansichten aus Deutschland* (pp. 189–194). Frankfurt a. M.: Peter Lang GmbH Europäischer Verlag der Wissenschaften.

Becker, G. S. (1981). *A treatise on the family*. Cambridge: Harvard University Press.

Becker, G. S. (1986). *Familie, Gesellschaft und Politik—die ökonomische Perspektive*. (deutsche Übersetzung) Tübingen: Mohr.

Becker, G. S., & Murphy, K. M. (2000). *Social economics. Market behavior in a social environment*. Cambridge: The Belknap Press of Harvard University Press.

Becker, G. S., & Posner R. A. (2009). *Uncommon sense: Economic insights, from marriage to terrorism*. Chicago: University of Chicago Press.

Caldwell, J, & Schindlmayr, T. (2003). Explanation of fertility crisis in modern societies: A search for commonalities. *Population Studies. A Journal of Demography, 57*(3), 241–263.

Cigno, A. (1991). *The economics of the family*. Oxford: Clarendon Press.

De Bruijn, B. J. (2005). Fertility: Theories, frameworks, models, concepts. In G. Caselli, J. Vallin, & G. Wunsch (Eds.), *Analysis and synthesis. A treatise in population studies* (Vol. 1, pp. 549–567). Amsterdam: Elsevier Academie Press.

Dondrich, K. O. (2007). *Weniger sind mehr*. Frankfurt a. M.: Campus Verlag.

Gensicke, T. (1996). Modernisierung, Wertewandel und Mentalitätsentwicklung in der DDR. In H. Bertram, S. Hradil, & G. Kleinhenz (Eds.), *Sozialer und demographischer Wandel in den neuen Bundesländern* (pp. 101–140). Opladen: Leske+Budrich.

Gensicke, T. (1998). *Die neuen Bundesbürger. Eine Transformation ohne Integration*. Opladen: Westdeutscher Verlag GmbH.

Hufnagel, R. (2002). Die Kosten von Kindern und die Kosten einer egalitären Partnerschaft. *Vierteljahreshefte zur Wirtschaftsforschung, 71*(1), 114–125. (Berlin: DIW).

Huinink, J. (1995). *Warum noch Familie? Zur Attraktivität von Partnerschaft und Elternschaft in unserer Gesellschaft*. Frankfurt a. M.: Campus Verlag.

Huinink, J., & Konietzka, D. (2003). Lebensformen und Familiengründung. Nichteheliche Elternschaft in Ost- und Westdeutschland in den 1990er Jahren. In W. Bien & J. H. Marbach (Eds.), *Partnerschaft und Familiengründung. Ergebnisse der dritten Welle des Familien-Survey* (pp. 65–93). Opladen: Leske+Budrich.

Humboldt, W. von. (1991). *Ideen zu einem Versuch, die Grenzen der Wirksamkeit des Staates zu bestimmen. Mit einem Nachwort von Robert Haerdter*. Stuttgart: Philipp Reclam jun.

Lechner, M. (1998). Eine empirische Analyse des Geburtenrückgangs in den neuen Bundesländern aus der Sicht der neoklassischen Bevölkerungsökonomie. *Zeitschrift für Wirtschafts- und Sozialwissenschaften; Vierteljahresheft der Gesellschaft für Wirtschafts- und Sozialwissenschaften—Verein für Socialpolitik, 118*(3), 463–468.

Lutz-Bachmann, M. (2011). *Humboldt—Ideal der Humnanität und die humanistische Bildungsreform*. Munich: Wissenmia GmbH.

McKenzie, R. B., & Tullock, G. (1984). *Homo oeconomicus. Ökonomische Dimensionen des Alltags; genehmigte Übersetzung d. engl.-sprachigen Orig.-Ausg. durch Jürgen Backhaus u. Friedrich Schneider*. Frankfurt a. M.: Campus Verlag.

Meulemann, H. (1998). Einleitung: Wertunterschiede zwischen West- und Ostdeutschland—Fakten und Erklärungsmöglichkeiten. In H. Meulemann (Ed.), *Werte und nationale Identität im vereinten Deutschland. Erklärungsansätze der Umfrageforschung* (pp. 7–21). Opladen: Leske+Budrich.

Rheinbay-Lehmann, B. (1998). *Frauen in den neuen Bundesländern: Auswirkungen der wirtschaftlichen und politischen Einheit auf die Situation der weiblichen Bevölkerung Thüringens*. Frankfurt a. M.: Peter Lang GmbH Europäischer Verlag der Wissenschaften.

Rosenzweig, B. (2002). Opfer, Verliererinnen, ungleiche Schwestern? In H. G. Wehling (Ed.), *Deutschland Ost—Deutschland West. Eine Bilanz* (pp. 178–198). Opladen: Leske+Budrich.

Scheuerer, G. (2010). *Wendeschock oder Babystreik? Die lexikographische Nutzenfunktion des Fertilitätsverhaltens*. Hanau: Haag+Herchen.

Schimany, P. (2003). *Die Alterung der Gesellschaft. Ursachen und Folgen des demographischen Umbruchs*. Frankfurt a. M.: Campus Verlag.

Schirrmacher, F. (2004). *Das Methusalemkomplott* (19th ed.). München: Karl Blessing Verlag GmbH.

Staatliche Zentralverwaltung für Rechnungsführung und Statistik der DDR (1). Statistical Yearbook of the GDR, several years; Central State Administration of Bookkeeping and Statistics of the German Democratic Republic, Berlin.

Statistisches Bundesamt (2001). *Statistical Yearbook for the Federal Republic of Germany, several years*. (Federal Statistical Office Germany. Wiesbaden). Stuttgart: (in the last years) Metzler-Poeschel.

Thüringer Allgemeine (2004). Thüringen sieht alt aus. Abwanderung: Studie prognostiziert im Freistaat höchsten Altersdurchschnitt aller Bundesländer and of 30th of April 2004: Aderlass ohne Ende. Immer mehr junge Menschen verlassen Thüringen—die Folgen könnten verheerend für den Freistaat sein.

Thüringer Landesamt für Statistik (1). *Statistisches Jahrbuch, several years*. Erfurt: Thüringer Landesamt für Statistik.

Thüringer Landesamt für Statistik (2003). *Statistischer Bericht: Ausgewählte Merkmale zur Entwicklung in Thüringen 1991–2002—Ergebnis des Mikrozensus*. Erfurt: Thuringian State Statistical Office.

Thüringer Landesamt für Statistik (2011). *Statistischer Bericht: Haushalte und Familien in Thüringen 2010—Ergebnisse des Mikrozensus*. Erfurt: Thuringian State Statistical Office.

Uth, J. (2000). *Laufende Verdiensterhebung im Produzierenden Gewerbe, Handel, Kredit- und Versicherungsgewerbe—Oktober 1995 bis Oktober 1999. Thüringer Landesamt für Statistik: Statistische Monatshefte Thüringen, 8/2000* (pp. 23–32). Erfurt: Thuringian State Statistical Office.

What Remains of Humboldt at Times of the Bologna Reform?

Hans A. Frambach

1 Introduction

What is the current situation at universities? Since the 1960s we observe a "massification of higher education" (Gibbons et al. 1994, pp. 76–80) with an increasing number of those passing school exams choosing their ways into universities. Nowadays, however, graduating from a university does not guarantee getting a job and is not sufficient condition to earn life's necessities. That means, the trade-off between the political aim, granting a maximum amount of education to the greatest possible number of people, and securing so-called "employability" of graduates, cannot be ignored. Adding to this are factors like tighter budgets of public households and the abolishment of university fees in Germany, further diminishing the means to handle and finance the student masses and calling for compliance to criterions of economic performance like efficiency. Furthermore, the low attractiveness especially of German degrees for foreign students was referred to as a reason to orient university training in Germany more strongly along international degree standards, the well-known bachelor and master's degrees. In connection to this, the international competitiveness of German university degrees was analyzed and goals were suggested to alleviate the university system by shortening study lengths, reducing the number of drop-outs, and attaining lower ages at career entry.

Necessitated by social and economic changes, demands and requirements like these stand behind the keyword "Bologna." Most of these current complaints, by the way, are not new: sub-financing of universities, overcrowded lecture rooms and courses, the insecure situation of following generations in science, the overload of teaching, etc., were already hotly debated issues in 1900 (Paletschek 2007, p. 15). The aims of European education policy are expressed in the "Bologna Declaration," the joint statement by the European Secretaries of Education from 1999.

H. A. Frambach (✉)
Department of Economics, Microeconomics and the History of Economic Thought,
Schumpeter School of Business & Economics, University of Wuppertal, Gaußstraße 20,
42119 Wuppertal, Germany
e-mail: frambach@wiwi.uni-wuppertal.de

J. G. Backhaus (ed.), *The University According to Humboldt*,
SpringerBriefs in Economics 89, DOI 10.1007/978-3-319-13856-5_4

In this paper I will not discuss the arguments of the critics of Humboldt's view of education as the perfect example of an elitist idea of education from which every empirical basis has been withdrawn since the professionalization of the professions of the late nineteenth century, or at the latest with the arrival of the mass university in the 1960s (e.g., Schulze 2005, p. 1). Also, I will not talk about the gigantic organizational obstacles that had to be overcome in implementing the bachelor and master's courses. Rather, this paper reflects my conviction that every kind of university-related education should include elements of educational experience that exceed those of mere professional training. This is not meant to imply that university training should not consider professional qualification—on the contrary: it is all about employability *and* education.

In the following the aims of Bologna shall briefly be presented. After this, Wilhelm von Humboldt's image of science will be outlined and a short impression of his concept of education is given. In a third step, central contradictions between Bologna and Humboldt are pointed out, without portraying this much discussed dispute in detail. Finally, the question is asked if the basic objectives of Humboldt can also be important in the Bologna era.

2 The Bologna Reform

Starting with the "Bologna-Declaration" and its most important aims, in the release text as of June 19, 1999 we read:

- Adoption of a system of easily readable and comparable degrees, also through the implementation of the Diploma Supplement, in order to promote European citizens employability and the international competitiveness of the European higher education system;
- Adoption of a system essentially based on two main cycles, undergraduate and graduate. Access to the second cycle shall require successful completion of first cycle studies, lasting a minimum of 3 years. The degree awarded after the first cycle shall also be relevant to the European labor market as an appropriate level of qualification. The second cycle should lead to the master and/or doctorate degree as in many European countries;
- Establishment of a system of credits—such as in the European credit transfer and accumulation system—as a proper means of promoting the most widespread student mobility. Credits could also be acquired in non-higher education contexts, including lifelong learning, provided they are recognized by the receiving universities concerned;
- Promotion of mobility by overcoming obstacles to the effective exercise of free movement with particular attention to:
  - For students, access to study and training opportunities and to related services;
  - For teachers, researchers and administrative staff, recognition and valorisation of periods spent in a European context researching, teaching, and training, without prejudicing their statutory rights;

- Promotion of European co-operation in quality assurance with a view to developing comparable criteria and methodologies;
- Promotion of the necessary European dimensions in higher education, particularly with regards to curricular development, inter-institutional co-operation, mobility schemes and integrated programmes of study, training and research (Bologna Declaration 1999, p. 8).

The aims of the Bologna declaration are not new and can be traced to reports of the European Round Table of Industrialists (ERT), an informal forum of executive boards from among the largest European industry and commercial enterprises, in the years 1989 and 1995. The central idea in these reports was that a university could decrease costs of education for firms if it expressed more "openness" concerning the introduction of new methods of treating human resources, and considering the needs of firms to a greater extent.[1] These reports were taken up by the European Commission by the end of 1995. In the same year, the World Bank published a report on finance problems in college education and favorably voiced recommendations for investments by the private sector. The Organization for Economic Co-operation and Development did similarly 1 year later.

Of course there were prominent advocates of the reform, mentioning only Burton R. Clark (1998), Michael Gibbons, and Helga Nowotny (e.g. Gibbons et al. 1994; Nowotny et al. 2002). The central idea of these scientists is that formerly, university, economy, science and technological applications were comparably independent of each other, whereas today, scientists and practitioners focused on interdisciplinarity and mobility. Systems of knowledge organization had to take economic and social interests much more into consideration which would, naturally, reduce the claim on autonomy by university and research to zero. Gibbons trenchantly formulated: "If the universities do not adapt, one has to manage without them." In other words: application-oriented research and knowledge build the future of university education (de Montlibert 2008, p. 35).

The previous university system was criticized for being, for example, too inflexible and inefficient, too slow regarding changes, and regarding the transfer and practical application of knowledge as being completely incapable (Schultheis et al. 2008, p. 9). To make teaching and research profitable, the costs for universities needed to be reduced, the advantages of the division of labor used, or, to put it more briefly, economic thinking and behavior needed to be introduced into university policy and organization. These demands were supported by the growing number of students and their changing educational requirements, as well as the difficulties of financing more staff in teaching, etc. (de Montlibert 2008, p. 29). Issuing a joint declaration on the harmonization of the architecture of the European higher education system in Sorbonne in May 1998 (Keller 2008, p. 48, 61), the four Secretaries in charge for France, Germany, Italy, and the UK spoke about the creation of a new "Europe of Knowledge." This new Europe of Knowledge, a market for European education—as of today still waiting to come into being—was already reduced by

[1] ERT, Education for Europeans. Towards the Learning Society, Brussels, March 1996 and ERT, Education and European Competence, Brussels, January 1999 (http://www.ert.de).

the ministers in Bologna in 1999 to the integration of citizens into a European labor market and the improvement of economic performance of Europe in the face of global competition (Keller 2008, p. 48). Visible features primarily are the standardization and quantification of knowledge, being based on the assumption that training and education are an entity with a measurable volume. This volume generates itself through work, understood as time invested in studies. According to this logic, 1 year of studies, as is commonly known, produces 60 credits (Keller 2008, p. 49)—the obvious and surely not intended parallels to the Ricardian and Marxist theory of labor value shall not be examined further here.

3 What Did Wilhelm von Humboldt Want?

Citing the political scientist and present chairwoman of the "German Society for the Investigation of the Political Intellect," Barbara Zehnpfennig (2010, p. 124), the question I would like to ask is: "If the Bologna process is the farewell to Humboldt," as is being said so often, what was it, then, that Wilhelm von Humboldt, the great reformer of the Prussian education system, founder of the University of Berlin and the neo-humanistic academic high school [neuhumanistisches Gymnasium], demanded for universities? Humboldt's list of requirements itself reads like a criticism of Bologna.

According to Humboldt, man has to look for something, "something, which, as a last goal, he can subordinate everything else to, and to which, as an absolute standard, he can judge everything." This he cannot find anywhere else than "within himself,… it therefore can exist only in his inner values, in his higher perfection." (Humboldt 1797a, p. 60). This "something inside," which has to be chosen, is nothing but the "dignity of man" (Humboldt 1797a, p. 60). The way leading to that goal is by education around the "mental life of people" [geistiges Leben der Menschen] (Humboldt 1810, p. 83). That means, the primary goal for Humboldt is not the qualification for a profession, not the acquisition of competences and abilities with the aim to climb up the social hierarchy, but the education of the individual (e.g., Menze 1985, p. 383). Only an individual thus formed can discuss matters of state, society, and constitution critically, and is thus able to contribute to their further progress. Hence, education has nothing to do with professional qualification or struggle for privileged positions (Wagner 1995, p. 62). In the words of the American sociologist Andrew Abott: "The reality is that education is a quality of presence of the self, a way of being in the moment. That quality, though, is a goal in its own right because it expands our present experience and hence is worthwhile in itself" (Abbott 2002, p. 20).

In accordance with Humboldt, education therefore is educating oneself—not in the sense of unbridled self-realization but as the cultivation of the self, of an unmistakable individuality. In this way human dignity and individuality arise as the result of a highest effort—hence, individuality is not something that is given to someone and not attainable for everyone, either. Of course, this contradicts the democratic assumption of individuality as something naturally possessed by an individual (Zehnpfennig 2010, pp. 126–127), and it led Humboldt to be accused of promoting the elites and his educational system of providing the justification for selection. This reproach is, of course, only comprehensible to a certain extent, because self-education, dignity, individuality, and social consciousness are—at least *as well*—the result of learning processes. Indeed, one could ask, if an individual who has been educated in von Humboldt's sense can nowadays really serve as an example to those who never ran through such processes of education, and whether such an exemplary function ever existed at all.

The route to that "human inside" is the objective of Humboldt's comparative anthropology with its primary aim of knowledge of the character. By "character" of man Humboldt understands "what moves in the soul, his thoughts, feelings, inclination and decisions, and how and in which consequence and combination they work—the relationship and the movement of his strengths, at once and thought as unity." [das Verhältnis und die Bewegung seiner Kräfte, zugleich und als Eins gedacht] (Humboldt 1797b, p. 453). The combination of the particular, of thoughts, feelings, inclination and decisions to unity make the character and with that the individual.

However, how are education and the educational system connected? Examining Humboldt's complete concept of education as a whole, the line followed from elementary school up to the university is science: science exists for education's sake, and education completes itself in science; the steps before it are steps leading to it. And even though only few people can reach that aim, they all benefit, according to their education, from the aim insofar that the aim reacts upon the way. The social utility of education and science is not to be neglected, though, emerging once it is released. However, the primary benefit of science is in the distinctive individuality created by the process of self-education.

Going back to the beginning of the nineteenth century, there are the so-called "manuscripts of ideas" [Ideenschriften], also by authors other than Humboldt who later contributed to the legendary reputation of the so-called "classic German" or "Humboldtian University"—though the two of them are not necessarily the same.[2] These manuscripts of ideas had a significant influence on the founding of the University of Berlin in 1810. One famous volume of these manuscripts of ideas was written by the Protestant theologian, philosopher, state theorist and educationalist Friedrich Daniel Ernst Schleiermacher (1768–1834), the "Casual thoughts on universities according to its meaning in German" ["Gelegentliche Gedanken über Universitäten in deutschem Sinn"], of 1808. With this document Schleiermacher intruded on a planning discussion for a new Prussian regional university in Berlin, originally raised by cabinet councilor Carl Friedrich von Beyme in 1806 at

[2] The Berlin historian of science Rüdiger vom Bruch (1999, p. 34) points out that the two main elements of "classical" German university—meaning the entrance of research into the university in the form of explorative teaching as well as the simultaneous shaping of a system of modern, systematic-methodical scientific branches—do not necessarily have to agree with the idea of the "Humboldtian university."

royal behest, by asking leading scholars (among them Wolf, Hufeland, Schmalz, and Fichte) to present well-founded plans (Böhm 2011, p. 519). Schleiermacher denoted his thoughts as casual and distinguished consciously them from two other and more extensive outlines: Schelling's extensive "Lectures on the method of academic studies" ["Vorlesungen über die Methode des akademischen Studiums"] and, first of all, Fichte's "Deduced plan to set up a higher educational institution in Berlin" ["Deduzierter Plan in einer in Berlin zu errichtenden höheren Lehranstalt"].

Schleiermacher speaks about "universities according to German meaning" [Universitäten im deutschen Sinn] and with that sets himself into stark contrast to the French university reform which, recently before that, had refuted general academic education and—because of the foundation of the Universitè Impériale in 1808 according to the model of strict educational centrism—preferred an education specialized according to disciplines (Paulsen 1902, p. 63, see also Huber 1960, pp. 286–287). With the phrase "according to German meaning," Schleiermacher explicitly alluded to Kant's "the quarrel of the faculties" ["Der Streit der Fakultäten"] from 1798—the writing that had opened the discussion about the reform of the universities which, until then, had been instrumentalized for state purposes—and at the same time demanded the creation of universities as a new idea that originated in philosophy (Böhm 2011, pp. 519–520).

Schleiermacher understands the idiom "according German meaning" primarily as the construction of the scientific educational passage in three steps: the succession of school, university, and academy. Metaphorically speaking, school is the meeting of masters and students, at university of masters and skilled workers, and in academy of masters among themselves (Schleiermacher 2000, p. 112). Behind this formula stands Schleiermacher's and also Schelling's and Fichte's, though differently accentuated, deep conviction of the fundamental unity and the general connection of all knowledge.

This German uniqueness in the allocation of school, university, and academy consequently forms the center of Humboldt's educational reform, and is not only in accordance with Schleiermacher's thoughts but also identifies Schleiermacher as the most influential among all the creative minds that were instrumental in building the new university in Berlin. After all, Schleiermacher was a founding dean of the theological faculty and a longstanding member of the so-called facilities commission [Einrichtungskommission] (Böhm 2011, pp. 520–521; Fallon 1980, pp. 32–36). A look aside Humboldt's famous education documents ("Theorie der Bildung des Menschen" ["Theory of the education of man "], 1793, "Über den Geist der Menschheit" ["On the spirit of mankind"], 1797, "Ideen zu einem Versuch, die Gränzen der Wirksamkeit des Staats zu bestimmen" ["Ideas for an attempt to determine the boundaries of the effectiveness of the state"], 1792) shows two reports Humboldt wrote in the summer of 1809 in his official function as educational reformer, namely, as director of the section for culture and teaching [Cultus und Unterricht] in the Prussian Home Office to which he was appointed in February 1809. One report, "Der Königsberger Schulplan" ["The Königsberg school plan"], 1809, was written in preparation of a conference for the improvement of the school system in Königsberg, the second one, "Der Litauische Schulplan" ["The Lithuanian school plan"], 1809, during an inspection trip in Lithuania (Humboldt 1809a, b).

Both school plans agree in providing three types of lessons [Unterricht] within the educational system: elementary lessons [Elementarunterricht], school lessons [Schulunterricht], and university lessons [Universitätsunterricht] (Humboldt 1809a, p. 70, b, p. 79). For Humboldt, and even for Schleiermacher and the other neo-humanist university reformers, elementary teaching is wrongly called lesson [Unterricht], because it actually just prepares the ground for lessons by imparting elementary cultural techniques such as reading and writing, numbers and measures, and speaking the mother tongue. Hence, by this step pupils are enabled to attend the school lessons that follow (Humboldt 1809a, p. 70, b, p. 79). School lessons introduce the pupil to mathematics, language, and history up to the point where it gets useless to further tie him to the teacher and to lessons; school lessons gradually free the pupil from the teacher because the teacher teaches the pupil what a teacher can teach. The pupil learns the ability to acquire knowledge by himself and this is a prerequisite for scientific insights (Humboldt 1809a, pp. 70–71; b, p. 79).

Humboldt speaks about lessons as concerns the university—there is hardly any connection to elementary teaching. In agreement with all the fundamental writings on education, and in particular with Fichte's educational concept, Humboldt states that the appropriation of a large quantities of knowledge, of learning how to learn, are no longer the objective of the university. The university lesson enables the former pupil to understand the unity of science beyond the mass of single pieces of knowledge and, furthermore, to enrich science creatively by using his productive rather than his receptive strengths. Elementary teaching had made the teacher possible, but he has been rendered dispensable by good school lessons so that at the university teachers do no longer meet learners, but masters meet "skilled workers" who work together in a common effort, the progress of science. As Humboldt writes: "It is left up to the university what man can find only through and into himself, the insight into pure science. Necessary for this self-act in the most real intellect is liberty, and helpful is solitude, and from these two points flow the whole outer organization of the universities. Listening to lectures is not important; it is essential to live in a narrow community with like-minded people who are of the same age, and to be aware of spending some years in a place of science with already perfectly educated people who dedicate their life to the rise and spreading of science"[3] (Humboldt 1809b, p. 79).

Therefore, University and school have quite different tasks whose separation, in Humboldt's opinion, must be carefully maintained (Humboldt 1810, p. 83).

[3] "Der Universität ist vorbehalten, was nur der Mensch durch und in sich selbst finden kann, die Einsicht in die reine Wissenschaft. Zu diesem Selbstakt [SelbstActus] im eigentlichsten Verstand ist notwendig Freiheit, und hilfreich Einsamkeit, und aus diesen beiden Punkten fließt zugleich die ganze äußere Organisation der Universitäten. Das Kollegienhören ist nur Nebensache, das wesentliche, daß man in enger Gemeinschaft mit Gleichgestimmten und Gleichaltrigen und dem Bewußtsein, daß es am gleichen Ort eine Zahl schon vollendet Gebildeter gebe, die sich nur der Erhöhung und Verbreitung der Wissenschaft widmen, eine Reihe von Jahren sich und der Wissenschaft lebe."

4 Inconsistencies between Bologna and Humboldt and Treatment of the Question Whether Basic Objectives/Ideals of Wilhelm von Humboldt Could be Kept Alive Even in the Bologna Era?

First of all one has to note that the educational reforms of the nineteenth century, including those that were executed with Humboldt as section leader in The Prussian Home Office, do not contain any specific element of Humboldt's ideas. Measures like the re-establishment and expansion of schools, the professionalization of teacher-training, etc. in first half of the nineteenth century, which are often represented as a feature of the success and consequence of Humboldt's reforms, must be understood as a result of the Prussian Civil Code rather than Humboldt's theory of education (vom Brocke 1981, p. 69; Huber 1960, pp. 280–281). Cologne education expert Clemens Menze (1985, p. 383) writes: "Accepting Wilhelm von Humboldt's concept of the organization of gradual education as arising from itself, his ideas are neither adapted by his contemporaries nor by the followers of the comprehensive school of later periods, including the advocates of integrated schools of our days. His organizational outline is substituted by a developing trinomial school system of great historical impact, which is based on other prerequisites, and pursues other aims than Humboldt's education concept allows."[4] Even in debates on school reform the name Humboldt does not play role (Menze 1985, p. 391). The drastic university reforms between 1790 and 1830 in the different German states were also primarily oriented toward the reform Universities of Göttingen and Halle rather than following the example of the University of Berlin founded in 1810 (Paletschek 2002, p. 184). To implement these reforms the state chose means that are in stark contrast to Humboldt (abandoning autonomous self-administration, rationalization, introduction of new subjects and courses of study, etc.) (Paletschek 2007, p. 12).

Humboldt's reputation is largely based on the reform process he helped to initiate and sustain, as well as on some of his ideas on the concept of the university and of higher education (Henningsen 2006, p. 95). Furthermore, his name is often associated with some general principles of German universities that led to the notion of the "Humboldtian University,", although this refers only to some of Humboldt's ideas (Fallon 1980, p. 10)—of course, *the* Humboldtian University never existed (Weingart 2010, p. 252). Although not explicitly stated in Humboldt's writings, the fundamental principles that lead to the term "Humboldtian University" (Weingart 2010, p. 251) are: the unity of research and teaching also in education instead of a pure knowledge transfer; the connection of technical education and general human education; finally, the community of scholars with equal rights (vom Bruch 1999,

[4] "Wilhelm von Humboldts in der Bildungsstruktur selbst fundierter Bildungsorganisationsentwurf nach Stufen wird weder zu seiner Zeit noch von den Einheitsschulanhängern der Folgezeit und den Gesamtschulaposteln unserer Tage rezipiert. An seine Stelle tritt zum einen ein sich herausbildendes und große geschichtliche Wirksamkeit entfaltendes dreigliedriges Schulsystem, das in anderen Voraussetzungen gründet und andere Ziele verfolgt als es Humboldts Bildungskonzept zulässt."

pp. 34–35). These principles secure the intellectual freedom of teaching and learning ["Lehrfreiheit" and "Lernfreiheit"] (Wittrock 2006, p. 112).

Nowadays, the break from a tradition of encyclopedic science and an orientation toward the principle of research are ideas connected with Humboldt, containing both science as something that was never found to be complete and never can be found to be so, but still to continually seek that which can never be completed (Humboldt 1810, p. 84). Nothing but a principle of the permanent quest for something new can be read from this famous thought in Humboldt's memorandum "Über die innere und äußere Organisation der höheren wissenschaftlichen Anstalten in Berlin" ["On the inner and outer organization of the higher scientific institutions in Berlin"].

Taking up the separation of school and university according to Humboldt and comparing this with Bologna, we see that in Bologna the significance of the school increases, while the importance of the university is being diminished into something like school (Zehnpfennig 2010, p. 124). The bachelor phase in particular is all about the acquisition of knowledge rather than a creative production of science. Today, even in master studies the realization of a productive as opposed to a receptive approach, as demanded for the university by Humboldt, can probably not be realized in most cases. The university no longer is the center of science and hardly reflects Humboldt's idea of education as an opportunity of an individual development of personality through science (vom Bruch 1999, p. 36). Rather, the university is a mixture of forcing-house, management head office and science administration. Increasingly, scientific results are merely presented to students, little time is available to communicate the ways of how to get the results. Therefore, students can at best portray the knowledge presented but hardly judge it critically. Mediocrity, always signified by a reduction in standards, becomes the measure of things. However, the Bologna reform is a response to the university for masses. Higher graduate numbers with shorter residence time at the university are politically desired. Yet, higher numbers of graduates also imply that other social strata participate in the university, namely those with lower educational achievements and lesser educational goals. This means, vocational orientation is at the center and not the experience of scientific work. The Bologna process thus achieves a politically desired leveling (Zehnpfennig 2010, p. 123).

A direct comparison of the positions of Humboldtians and Bologneses can perhaps best be outlined by the catchphrase "education by science" vs. "education for professions," referring to professions in enterprises of all branches, public administration, hospitals, schools, law courts, newspapers, etc. (Schimank 2009, p. 18). Undoubtedly, education for its own sake plays an ever decreasing role at universities. The organizing principle in alignment with a harmonious education of all capabilities of man has given way to the importance of certain contents for life in the modern world (Menze 1985, p. 388). The reproach of practice orientation and a turning of some university-related contents into the direction of universities of applied sciences can certainly not be rejected. Political educational reporting calculates "educational returns," demonstrating that practice orientation pays off; after all, having passed exams, 90 % of graduates pursue careers outside science and research (Schimank 2009, p. 19).

On the other hand, education fulfills Humboldt's view of openness toward the future instead of immediate practice-oriented knowledge. For Humboldt it is "living, creative strengths" ["lebendige, schaffende Kräfte"] that keep the process of education open and permanently give rise to something new. Spontaneity and creativity could also be regarded as immanent components of behavior and education. This means that education may not be related one-sidedly to the present world including their present problems. Rather, it is to train competences which refer to the moments of creativity and future openness (Wagner 1995, p. 85). This is a necessary realization in the course of the Bologna process, and another one maybe that the original intentions of Bologna would possibly be better and more sustainably supported by Humboldt's opinion.

The crucial part of the Prussian university reform at the beginning of the nineteenth century was the new establishment of philosophical faculties, which meant institutionalizing philosophical reflection as an indispensable moment of science within the other disciplines. Humboldt identified the general quality of philosophy in the context of philosophizing within the individual sciences. It was not intended to add another individual faculty or even a faculty for prospective teachers to the existing faculties for theology, jurisprudence, and medicine (Benner 2003, p. 218). Modern standards of expenditure by the state have no room for the idea of connecting the contents of different faculties, embodied, for example, in the philosophy of science as a branch of philosophy. Concerning university planning, the state nowadays, as mentioned above, is oriented at interests of economic utilization. However, this does not only directly contradict Humboldt's basic idea that the state may not interfere in science. In accordance with Humboldt, the state has to provide the financial resources, and it has to do this in a way that "the mental and the exalted" ["das Geistige und Hohe"] are not pulled down to "material and humble reality" ["materielle und niedere Wirklichkeit"] (Humboldt 1810, p. 83). The state is not allowed to demand anything from the university that could confer a direct advantage. On the contrary, "from a much higher point of view" the university will fulfill the objectives of the state anyway, if the liberty of the universities remains untouched (Humboldt 1810, p. 83). If we watch the cuts and sometimes closures in the areas of the sociological and philosophical faculties during the last years, then the contradictions to Humboldt's idea are clearly revealed. An impression that should not arise, of course, is that Humboldt understood it as the state's natural task to provide cost-free education for everyone, including studying at the university. His position rather corresponded to those of the old Greek philosophers, for example, he deeply admired Plato (Fallon 1980, p. 22).

5 Summary and Conclusions

Starting point of the Bologna reforms was the conference of the European Secretaries of Education and Science in Bologna (1999) to decide on a common procedure in the science sector. Main goals were, first, the standardization of European higher education, not least to be reached by the realization of comparability of degrees, and second, connected to that, an increase in the mobility of students within Europe. Undisputedly, these aims do not touch study contents and subject, they only relate to the superficial structure, that means a comparable structure of studies and comparable degrees. Of course, originating from this change of structure, serious effects on the contents of study began to emerge, the standardization of country-specific cultural knowledge (Zehnpfennig 2010, p. 122).

The university is deeply concerned with the question of professional suitability of courses of studies and the increased bureaucratic effort accompanied by the Bologna process (increasing examinations, evaluations, outline of conditions of study, credit point administration, etc.), developments that dramatically diminish the time for research and teaching. Important promises by the instatement of bachelor degrees are not fulfilled at all: the mobility of the students remains more or less unchanged, drop-out rates are still high, duration of study is still long, the alleged professional qualification is often questioned, and this not only by college lecturers but primarily by enterprises (Wuggenig 2008, p. 149; for current developments in Germany, see Heublein et al. 2012, Chaps. 3–5).

Education and science are of excellent and high value, they seize and change the entire person, they may not be mistaken for the accumulation of knowledge and they may not be charged with immediate practical requirements. The state has the task to grant universities liberty and to protect them materially. If science is practiced in its own spirit, then it grants a much deeper utility than could ever be reached by superficial calculations of utility—this was clearly expressed by Wilhelm von Humboldt. Science is all about human education, not mere vocational training; it is all about the ability of the scientific intellect, not only knowledge accumulation; it is all about intellectual independence, not only reproduction and application of knowledge (Zehnpfennig 2010, p. 124).

Finally, it might be worthwhile to remind ourselves that education is the most decisive factor for improving the condition of our societies and economies. In this respect the question is not to undo the reform processes or to even deny its necessity but to bring the aims of professional ability and education into harmony. What we need is professional ability *and* education, not professional ability or education.

References

Abbott, A. (2002). Welcome to the University of Chicago. *Forschung und Lehre, 8/07.*

Benner, D. (2003). Wilhelm von Humboldts Bildungstheorie. Eine problemgeschichtliche Studie zum Begründungszusammenhang neuzeitlicher Bildungsreform (1st ed.). Weinheim: Juventa-Verlag.

Böhm, W. (2011). Über Universitäten in deutschem Sinn, Pädagogische Rundschau 5, 65. Jahrgang, September/Oktober, 65(5), 519–527.

Bologna Declaration. (1999). The Bologna Declaration on the European space for higher education: an explanation. http://ec.europa.eu/education/policies/educ/bologna/bologna.pdf. Accessed 21 March 2012.

Burton, R. C. (1998). Creating entrepreneurial universities: Organizational pathways of transformation. New York: Pergamon Press.

de Montlibert, C. (2008). Universitätsreform und Begriffspolitik. In F. Schultheis, P. -F. Cousin, & M. Roca i Escoda (Eds.), *2008. Humboldts Albtraum. Der Bologna-Prozess und seine Folgen* (pp. 29–46). Konstanz: UVK.

Fallon, D. (1980). *The German University, a heroic ideal in conflict with the modern world*. Boulder: Colorado Associated University Press.

Gibbons, M., Limoges, C., Nowotny, H., Schwarzman, S., Scott, P., & Trow, M. (1994). *The new production of knowledge: The dynamics of science and research in contemporary societies*. London: Sage.

Henningsen, B. (2006). A joyful good-bye to Wilhelm von Humboldt: The German University and the Humboldtian Ideals of "Einsamkeit and Freiheit". In K. Blückert, G. Neave, & T. Nybom (Eds.), *The European Research University. A historical parenthesis* (pp. 91–107). New York: Palgrave MacMillan.

Heublein, U., Richter, J., Schmelzer, R., & Sommer, D. (2012). Die Entwicklung der Schwund- und Studienabbruchquoten an den deutschen Hochschulen Statistische Berechnungen auf der Basis des Absolventenjahrgangs 2010. *HIS: Forum Hochschule, 3/2012*.

Huber, E. R. (1960). *Deutsche Verfassungsgeschichte seit 1789, Vol. I: Reform und Restauration 1789–1830*. Stuttgart: Kohlhammer.

Humboldt, W. von. (1797a). Über den Geist der Menschheit. In W. Flitner (Ed.), *1956. Wilhelm von Humboldt. Schriften zur Anthropologie und Bildungslehre* (pp. 59–67). Düsseldorf: Verlag Helmut Küpper.

Humboldt, W. von. (1797b). Das achtzehnte Jahrhundert. In W. von Humboldt (Ed.), *Collected Works in 5 Vols*. (Vol. I, pp. 376–505). Darmstadt: Wissenschaftliche Buchgesellschaft (1960).

Humboldt, W. von. (1809a). Der Königsberger Schulplan. In W. Flitner (Ed.), *1956. Wilhelm von Humboldt. Schriften zur Anthropologie und Bildungslehre* (pp. 69–76). Düsseldorf: Verlag Helmut Küpper.

Humboldt, W. von. (1809b). Der Litauische Schulplan. In W. Flitner (Ed.), *1956. Wilhelm von Humboldt. Schriften zur Anthropologie und Bildungslehre* (pp. 76–82). Düsseldorf: Verlag Helmut Küpper.

Humboldt, W. von. (1810). Über die innere und äußere Organisation der höheren wissenschaftlichen Anstalten in Berlin. In W. Flitner (Ed.), *1956. Wilhelm von Humboldt. Schriften zur Anthropologie und Bildungslehre* (pp. 82–90). Düsseldorf: Verlag Helmut Küpper.

Keller, F. (2008). Nomaden des wissenschaftlichen Feldes. Über die neue Geometrie des Wissens und die Kunst des Navigierens. In F. Schultheis, P. -F. Cousin, & M. Roca i Escoda (Eds.), *Humboldts Albtraum. Der Bologna-Prozess und seine Folgen* (pp. 47–62). Konstanz: UVK.

Menze, C. (1985). Ist die Bildungsreform Wilhelm von Humboldts gescheitert? In G. Heintz & P. Schmitter (Eds.), *Collectanea Philologica* (pp. 381–401). Baden Baden: Valentin Koerner.

Nowotny, H., Scott, P., & Gibbons, M. (2002). *Re-thinking science: Knowledge and the public in an age of uncertainty*. Cambridge: Polity Press.

Paletschek S. (2002). Die Erfindung der Humboldtschen Universität. Die Konstruktion der deutschen Universitätsidee in der ersten Hälfte des 20. Jahrhunderts. *Historische Anthropologie, 10*, 183–205.

Paletschek S. (2007). Zurück in die Zukunft? Universitätsreformen im 19. Jahrhundert. In W. Jäger (Ed.), *Das Humboldt-Labor: Experimentieren mit den Grenzen der klassischen Universität* (pp. 11–15). Freiburg: Albert Ludwig Universität.

Paulsen, F. (1902). *Die deutschen Universitäten und das Universitätsstudium*. Berlin: A. Asher.

Schimank, U. (2009). Humboldt in Bologna—falscher Mann am falschen Ort?, Opening Speech of the conference „Studienqualität" of the HIS Society, 25/26 March 2009, Hanover.

Schleiermacher, F. (2000). *Texte zur Pädagogik. Kommentierte Studienausgabe* (Vol. 1). Frankfurt a. M.: Suhrkamp.

Schultheis, F., Cousin, P.-F., & Roca i Escoda, M. (Eds.). (2008). *Humboldts Albtraum. Der Bologna-Prozess und seine Folgen*. Konstanz: UVK.

Schultheis, F., Cousin, P. -F., & Roca i Escoda, M. (2008). Konstruktion und Folgen eines europäischen Hochschulsystems. In F. Schultheis, P. -F. Cousin, & M. Roca i Escoda (Eds.), *2008. Humboldts Albtraum. Der Bologna-Prozess und seine Folgen* (pp. 7–16). Konstanz: UVK.

Schulze, W. (2005). *"Mit Humboldt nach Bologna!"—Grundfragen der Neuordnung von Studiengängen.* Zeitenblicke, *4*(1/2005), 1–8.

vom Brocke, B. (1981). Preußen—Land der Schulen, nicht nur der Kasernen. Preußische Bildungspolitik von Gottfried Wilhelm Leibniz und Wilhelm von Humboldt bis Friedrich Althoff und Carl Heinrich Becker (1700–1930). In W. Böhme (Ed.), *Preußen—eine Herausforderung, Herrenalber Texte (32)* (pp. 54–99). Karlsruhe: Boehme.

vom Bruch, R. (1999). Langsamer Abschied von Humboldt? Etappen deutscher Universitätsgeschichte 1810–1945. In M. G. Ash (Ed.), *Mythos Humboldt. Vergangenheit und Zukunft der deutschen Universitäten* (pp. 29–57). Vienna: Böhlau.

Wagner, H.-J. (1995). *Die Aktualität der strukturalen Bildungstheorie Humboldts.* Weinheim: Deutscher Studien Verlag.

Weingart, P. (2010). Humboldt im Ranking. In A. Schlüter & P. Strohschneider (Eds.), *Bildung? Bildung! 26 Thesen zur Bildung als Herausforderung im 21. Jahrhundert, Lizenzausgabe für die Landeszentrale für politische Bildung, NRW* (pp. 249–259). Berlin: Berlin Verlag.

Wittrock, B. (2006). The legacy of Wilhelm von Humboldt and the future of the European University. In K. Blückert, G. Neave, & T. Nybom (Eds.), *The European Research University. A historical parenthesis* (pp. 109–125). New York: Palgrave MacMillan.

Wuggenig, U. (2008). Eine Transformation des universitären Feldes: Der Bologna-Prozess in Deutschland und seine Vorgeschichte. In F. Schultheis, P. -F. Cousin, & M. Roca i Escoda (Eds.), *2008. Humboldts Albtraum. Der Bologna-Prozess und seine Folgen* (pp. 123–162). Konstanz: UVK.

Zehnpfennig, B. (2010). Demokratie und (Un-)Bildung: Platon, Humboldt und Bologna. *Synthesis Philosophica, 49*(1/2010), 121–130.

University Studies at Hardenberg's and Humboldt's Time and the Professionalization of University Studies Today

Karl-Heinz Schmidt

1 Two Hundred Years of University Studies and Education Policy in Germany

Since the end of the eighteenth century the academic education has undergone deep structural changes. Several areas of conflicts have risen during the past two centuries. At present the conflicts are linked to different levels of public administration and institutions of the education system. The most important areas of conflicts concern: (1) the objectives of education policy, (2) the coordination of education programs and activities of the institutions of the education system, (3) the orientation of professional schools, academies, and colleges to professional fields of education, (4) the orientation of universities, laboratories, and other institutions of higher education to programs of scientific research and/or to professional education. The nucleus of the conflict areas is incorporated in the relation of education programs of the different institutions.

This basic problem already developed when Karl August von Hardenberg (1750–1822) and Wilhelm von Humboldt (1767–1835) were studying at German universities, but it became more crucial for the long-term development of the universities during the late twentieth and beginning twenty-first century, especially in Germany. The decisive question thus will be: What are the German universities obliged to offer to the society: general academic education or special, profession-oriented knowledge? Is it necessary to integrate more professional education into the programs of university courses, or should specialized academies and professional colleges—"Fachhochschulen"—be responsible for professional higher education? The problem may also be exposed as follows: more integration or more

K.-H. Schmidt (✉)
Department of Economic Sciences, University of Paderborn, Warburger str. Nr. 100, 33098 Paderborn, North Rhine-Westphalia, Germany
Email: Karl-Heinz_Schmidt@notes.upb.de

J. G. Backhaus (ed.), *The University According to Humboldt*,
SpringerBriefs in Economics 89, DOI 10.1007/978-3-319-13856-5_5

specialization in the education system, beforehand in Germany, but probably in other European countries as well?

In order to orientate the following paragraphs to this problem, it is necessary to expose the former framework conditions of academic education. Two examples will be demonstrated: the studies of the students K.A. von Hardenberg and W. von Humboldt. Furthermore, the basic reforms of the education system must be considered, including W. von Humboldt's activities to realize the foundation of the University of Berlin. Moreover, the professionalization of university studies "today" must be pointed out, in order to emphasize the conflict of the universities between the orientation to general academic research and teaching and to practice-oriented, professionalized teaching. Therefore, the education activities of universities, academies, professional colleges ("Fachhochschulen"), and professional high schools should be taken into account. Conclusively, the historical framework of the following paragraphs considers the academic studies at the turn from the eighteenth to the nineteenth century and from the twentieth to the twenty-first century, especially in Germany.

Concerning the universities, the following characteristics of the long-term development of the academic institutions must be acknowledged (Weber 1922, pp. 524–555, especially p. 524 ff):

1. Periods of stagnation were followed by periods of reforms. Every reform should bring about new knowledge which could be put forward in opposition to the existing historical, decaying level of knowledge about "truth" (Schelsky 1963, p. 13).
2. In earlier centuries, universities were established as autonomous institutions, but in later centuries the autonomy was restricted by political and economic changes, in Germany strictly during the twentieth century (1933–1945). After the Second World War, the German universities started to strive for autonomy again, but only at the turn to the twenty-first century a new legislation was settled to stabilize the autonomy of the universities, except the financing ot the university budget.
3. The professionalization of education was not a definite objective of universities. During the middle ages, the academic degree was not a condition of access to professional practice, but a recommendation. During the twentieth century, the German universities were more directly orientated to general education, but to some extent also to professional education. In some states of Germany even special new colleges—"Hochschulen"—were established, in the state of North Rhine-Westphalia: "Gesamthochschulen" (Rau 1977; Fisch and Vollmer 1998).
4. The new area of conflict was developed by the changing structure of the education system: general academic education by autonomous universities orientated to research and teaching, or specialized teaching and related research at "Fachhochschulen" and academies. This problem is discussed continously.

2 Two Examples of University Students at German Universities

2.1 *Karl August von Hardenberg*

University students in Germany may look backwards to a long-term development of universities in Europe. They should realize that the first "universities" in Europe were formed on the grounds of special "schools" established by bishops of cathedrals, monasteries, or Latin schools. The history of universities also demonstrates, that the structure of academic degrees of university education dates back to the twelfth century and that the oldest German universities were founded in Prague (1348), Vienna (1365), Heidelberg (1386), Cologne (1389), Erfurt (1392), and Leipzig (1409) (Gerber 1959, p. 472). These "universities," yet, consisted of few faculties only: the "higher" faculties (theology, law, and medicine) and an "artist faculty" (for studies of Latin, logic, rhetorics, arithmetics, etc.), but which incorporated more students than the "higher" faculties—even at the fourteenth and fifteenth century.

Contrasting to the medieval time the structure of the German universities was changed definitely since the development of Protestantism, enlightenment, and natural science in Europe. New universities were founded, and new faculties with new curricula were started mainly during the seventeenth and eighteenth century. Examples are given by the universities of Halle (1694) and Göttingen (1734). The "artists faculty" was organized as an independent philosophical faculty performing academic rights equal to the rights of the "higher" faculties. Both universities were reorganized from church-oriented religiously based institutions offering general studies to "modern" universities performing enlighted programs of studies by public institutions, which were established not by churches or monasteries, but by the enlighted sovereign.

At such a "modern" university Karl August von Hardenberg started his studies of law since the winter semester 1766/1767: in Göttingen (Klausa 1990). As he was only 16 years old and as his family followed the customs, he was accompanied by a personal housekeeper and guard, the "Haushofmeister." This person, yet, motivated the young student to benefit more from leisure than from regular studies, though Karl August's field of studies did not only cover law, but also mathematics, natural sciences, antique history, and document science. The preferences for the broad studies were based on former advice by his uncle Friedrich Karl von Hardenberg, known as director of the royal gardens in Herrenhausen next to Hannover (Hermann 2003, p. 41; von Bothmer and Köhler 2011, p. 25; Stamm-Kuhlmann 2000, p. 86, 92 f). After four semesters of studies in Göttingen, Karl August changed his location: he continued his studies at the University of Leipzig. His fields were law and "belles lettres," painting and music. A new "Hofmeister" (Gervinus) accompanied him. Probably he also met or observed other (later on famous) students like Goethe, Lessing, and Winckelmann, but meetings with Goethe presumably were casual (Hermann 2003, p. 44). Hardenberg preferred irregular and erotic adventures which consumed his budget financed by his father (Hermann 2003, p. 45).

Since the summer semester 1769, Hardenberg continued his studies of law, history, and politics at the University of Göttingen. His academic teachers were especially Johann Stephan Pütter (private law of German princes), Johann Christoph Gatterer (history) and—as a less important teacher—Gottfried Achenwall (statistics). Hardenberg's more important teacher was Pütter, to whom the student developed a personal contact; the teacher even exposed his student as one of the most polite and talented young men (Hermann 2003, p. 50). After one more year of studies, altogether eight semesters in Göttingen, the student Hardenberg declared his studies to be finished. He did not need a final exam: His status as "Freiherr" enabled him to leave the university with this autonomous decision. But he succeeded to pass an exam at the judicial institution of the "Kurfürstentum" Hannover, though his first employment in the judicial administration (Justizkanzlei) in Hannover was arranged already by his father (Hermann 2003, p. 51).

Conclusively, the university studies at Hardenberg's time of studies were characterized by four factors:

1. High degree of autonomy how to spend the time for leisure and studies.
2. A personal servant (Haushofmeister) who accompanied and observed the student at the university location.
3. Free choice of the (broad) fields of studies.
4. No obligatory exams for students being members of the nobility (status) and no severe problems of finding employment after studies.

Another example of university students of the eighteenth century is given by Wilhelm von Humboldt. He also was member of the nobility benefitting from this social status.

2.2 *Wilhelm von Humboldt*

The first phase of school education of Wilhelm von Humboldt was performed by a private teacher, paid by the parents. Since 1777 their two sons—Wilhelm and Alexander—got lessons by a teacher for more than 10 years: Gottlob Johann Christian Knuth (Gall 2011, 21 f). He coordinated the lessons of several teachers who were specialized to certain fields of school education. Moreover, the two sons were prepared by private lecturers in different academic fields as economics, statistics, philosophy, and law. The teacher Knuth even became a loyal counselor and long-term friend of the family. He also took care of the two brothers, when they left their parents' home (1787), in order to study at the university. Wilhelm started studying sciences of law in Frankfurt (Oder); his brother Alexander entered the studies of the sciences of the state at the same university. But after one semester Wilhelm changed the university: he moved to Göttingen (Gall 2011, pp. 28–31). He also changed the structure of his studies: less emphasis on law, more involvement in philosophy, history, and antique languages. After four semesters of studies (1790), Humboldt started his professional career in the department of legislation

(Justizdepartement) to be educated to act as a judge. Simultaneously, Humboldt aimed at an additional qualification to be able to start a professional career in the diplomatic service of the state. One year later, yet, Humboldt quitted this professional status and changed his activities to study ancient languages, history, and culture—and to get married.

To conclude: Humboldt's studies at the university were characterized by:

1. Efficient studies mainly at the University of Göttingen.
2. Availability of a loyal long-term teacher, counselor, and coordinator of studies, obviously not only a "Haushofmeister," but a close friend of the family.
3. Orientation of studies to ancient languages, history, and culture.
4. Attempts to develop close personal contacts to famous academic teachers at the university (mainly in Göttingen: Johann Stephan Pütter, Georg Christoph Lichtenberg, Christian Gottlob Heyne, August Ludwig von Schlözer).

Humboldt changed his employment in the public administration and legislation (since 1790) several times (Gall 2011, 30 f).

3 Humboldt's Concept of Reforms of the Education-System in Prussia

3.1 Humboldt's Reform Procedure

Publications on Wilhelm von Humboldt's life and activities demonstrate, that the framework conditions of his activities changed more often and that his functions in politics and society differed extremely during the phases of his life. One of the functions concerned the reform of the education system in Prussia. The Prussian politician Freiherr vom und zum Stein had proposed as the first politician, that Humboldt should return from the position of a representative of the Prussian state at the Vatican in Rome (1801–1808) in order to accept the position of the director of a new section for culture and public schooling and education in Prussian public administration and cultural politics. On the grounds of this function—Humboldt assumed—he would get the opportunity to develop and to realize new ideas of future education as contributions to the re-ascent of the Prussian state after the military and political defeat by Napoleon (Gall 2011, 128 ff). In fact Humboldt was appointed to act as director of the new section of culture and public schooling and education since February 20, 1809, and immediately he got strictly involved into the new obligation. Lothar Gall describes Humboldt's activities in detail: at first he demanded exact reports about the objectives, financial situation, and responsibilities of each institution to set up a "general tableau" about the demand for subsidies in each institution of the schooling and education system.

Second, Humboldt tried to find out the ideas of employees of the section concerning their visions and opportunities of reforms. This practice of dialogues with colleagues involved in actual problems was one of Humboldt's strengths, in fact a "bottom-up approach." As he wrote in a letter, he preferred the ideas and proposals of the concerned group of collaborators instead of the ideas of individual persons, including his own opinion (Gall 2011, 140 f).

Third, Humboldt observed the collaborators to share the same basic ideas and objectives of education and culture. He found that the ideas of enlightenment, as they were proclaimed by Immanuel Kant, Christian Jakob Kraus, and Johann Gottfried Herder, determined those basic ideas. After having appointed the adequate persons on the grounds of these preparatory ideas and activities, Humboldt started his work focusing on the basic reform of all institutions of the concerned section, of which he was responsible. "Es ging, vor allen Einzelheiten, vor allen Reformschritten im Detail und in den Bereichen, um die leitenden Prinzipien …, kurz, um die Grundkonzeption des Ganzen" (Gall 2011, p. 145).

Fourth, Humboldt wrote down his ideas about the "Grundkonzeption" in a document comparable to a "Denkschrift," as it was practised in politics and administration at that time, also by Karl August von Hardenberg (see especially his "Rigaer Denkschrift," 1807). Though Humboldt's manuscript was a fragment, which was published only after his death (1851), it dealt with his basic ideas and visions of the reforms he had in mind: "Über die innere und äußere Organisation der höheren wissenschaftlichen Anstalten in Berlin" (Gall 2011, p. 146; dtv-Lexikon 10 2006, p. 79). Humboldt exposed "Höhere wissenschaftliche Anstalten" including two types of institutions: (1) universities, responsible for sciences and public lectures, which focused on the dialogue with young persons as actively thinking individuals ("mitdenkende Köpfe") orientated to common services on behalf of science; (2) academies, consisting of loose connections of an academic cooperative, by which academics find opportunities to prepare scientific manuscripts as authors in isolated leisure. Both institutions should be focused on services on behalf of the sciences. From this point of view, the difference between the tasks of the professor and the school teacher should be obvious: the teacher shall instruct pupils; the professor shall cooperate with his students to serve the aspiration for science and research. The state should be orientated to two objectives: (1) to keep the higher scientific institutions in vivid activities, and (2) to keep the higher institution separated from the school. As Lothar Gall concludes: according to Humboldt's concept the state should keep away from the central tasks and activities of universities and academies (Gall 2011, 148 f). Instead the state should take care of the appointment of strength and diversity of the staff of universities and academies and for the freedom of their activities. The state should be restricted to specific interventions at the universities, but the academies should benefit from a larger degree of liberty ("Freiraum"); the academy should be acknowledged as "the most independent Corporation," i.e. independent from the state (Gall 2011, 150).

Humboldt's concept, therefore, turned out to be oriented to the state of absolutism, but also to reforms of the state, especially in the field of schooling politics and education (Wikipedia 2012). The more concretely his statements and recommendations, yet, were exposed, the more strictly he acknowledged certain forms of interventions by the state mainly concerning the universities. These basic statements may be taken as a platform to refer to the concrete measures of Humboldt's cultural politics and reforms of the education system, especially to the foundation of the University of Berlin.

3.2 The Foundation of the University of Berlin: Economic and Academic Problems

After having selected the collaborators of the new section Humboldt orientated his first activity on the development of a general plan for the diverse forms of schools including curricula and basic principles of the methodology to be applied. Three consecutive types of schools should be established: elementary schools, high schools ("höhere Bürgerschule"), and advanced high schools ("gelehrte Schule" or "Gymnasium"). The "advanced high schools" were of special interest for Humboldt, because they should end by a final exam "Abitur." The schedule of the curricula had been programmed earlier than Humboldt's appointment as director of the new section. Freiherr vom Stein had pushed forward the plan to establish a special committee for this task: a scientific deputation ("wissenschaftliche Deputation"). But this attempt to realize a reform of the schooling system in Prussia was not carried on successfully. Instead of self-sustaining, independent citizens the reorganized schools were focused on loyal subjects (Duchhardt 2010, p. 46 ff).

Humboldt, yet, started several other reform projects. One of them concerned the foundation of the University of Berlin (Gerber 1959, p. 472 f). Though the relevant plans had been pursued prior to Humboldt's appointment—also von K. A. Hardenberg may have developed related ideas—Humboldt pushed the basic ideas and plans forward very strictly (Busch 2005). About half a year since he had been appointed, Humboldt demanded for the permission to establish the new university, and the Prussian King accepted the plans within 3 weeks (August 1809). He was very satisfied about this success, as the plans did not only concern the university, but also two academies, the library, museums, and an observatory. All of these institutions should be integrated in one large establishment. The King presented several buildings and financial funds as subsidies to the University of Berlin. Humboldt was proud and convinced, that the new establishment would be a model also for other universities, in Humboldt's own words:

> … für die Zukunft wurde ein großes Etablissement gegründet, das, wenn nur eine gutgesinnte Regierung bleibt, Epoche in Deutschland machen muß. (Brief von W. v. Humboldt an seine Frau Caroline, zitiert nach Gall 2011, p. 158 and 398, Footnote 161).

The only new foundation within this network was the University of Berlin.

The procedure of realizing the relevant ideas and plans demonstrated again the principles which Humboldt and his team of collaborators had in mind, when they started to set up the reform-oriented new academic institution (Gall 2011, p. 157 f). According to Humboldt's vision, the new university should be established in Berlin for two reasons: (1) Prussia was expected to reorganize schooling and education according to the principles of enlightenment and higher mental education. To pursue this obligation, the new university should be established at a central location, where other institutions for schooling and education already existed. (2) The establishment (a) after Prussia's defeat (b) at the central location and (c) in connection with other cultural and educational institutions at the same location (Berlin) should bring about a higher degree of diversity ("Mannigfaltigkeit") and a higher qualification of the academic staff and personnel of the total complex of the "higher institution of schooling and education." The new "allgemeine Lehranstalt" should be organized as an organic total unit ("organisches Ganzes"), not as separated faculties, and this new institution should be called "University," but without the negative effects of former universities (Gall 2011, 159 f).

These arguments point out economic problems as far as the organization of the new university is concerned. Furthermore, economic problems were linked with the ways of financing the new academic institutions. Herewith, Humboldt exposed specific ideas (Gall 2011, 162 f): elementary schools should be financed by communities, high schools by new provincial funds, universities and academies by receipts on the grounds of public property (domains), which should be transferred to the academic institutions; furthermore they should receive additional "contributions of the nation." This way of financing should bring about autonomy in relation to the state. Simultaneously, the academic problem of interventions by the state into the programs of teaching and research should be solved: autonomy should also be valid for the scientific institutions in relation to the state.

Humboldt was strongly interested to reduce the influence of the state following from absolutism on the institutions of the schooling and education, moreover on the social groups which strived for independent social development. Two political positions became obvious: (1) Representatives of a strong, independent state (see: Stein and Hardenberg), and (2) representatives of the "nation" as supreme institution in social and political development (Humboldt). The full conflict, yet, came about many years later, but it could be recognized already. The basic political position and objective of Wilhelm von Humboldt has been exposed by Lothar Gall very clearly:

> … Aufbau eines von der Nation getragenen Gemeinwesens, das den selbständigen Kräften innerhalb dieser Nation den weitestmöglichen Spielraum ließ. (Gall 2011, p. 166)

Apart from the financial problems the foundation of the University of Berlin was connected with academic problems. They mainly concerned the appointment of the teaching staff and the personnel for institutinal research and administration.

From the economic point of view, the organization of the total complex of involved institutions turned out to be a problem of cooperation and networking. The whole section of schooling and education should be organized according to cost efficiency and individual preferences orientated to individual independence and institutional autonomy. Humboldt's objectives, yet, should turn out to be opposed to the representatives of the strong monarchy. The conflict was prepared in Humboldt's earlier and Hardenberg's later motivation and strategy.

Summarizing Humboldt's reforms of the education system in Prussia at the beginning of the nineteenth century, the following points are to be emphasized:

1. Humboldt's attempt to set up reforms of the schooling and education system was based on a "bottom-up approach"; he tried to get involved his collaborators in the reform projects.
2. Humboldt strived for autonomy of universities and academies from interventions by the state; especially the academy should be understood as "the most independent Corporation"; the university might be influenced by restricted interventions of the state.
3. The University of Berlin was founded as a basic component of a complex of academic institutions, including two academies, a library, museums, and an observatory; the faculties should not separate the institutions strictly; instead, academic staff members of the academies should be appointed to teach at the University of Berlin, at least during the years after the foundation.

Humboldt's concept influenced the organization of schooling and scientific research not only in Prussia, but also in other German states and in neighbor countries. An example was pointed out during the discussion of this paper at the "Heilbronn Symposium" held in Heilbronn, June 2012. Mainly Gerrit Meijer, University of Maastricht, pointed out, why and how Humboldt's reform approach became effective in The Netherlands. According to additional information by Gerrit Meijer (e-mails June and July 2012) several sources should be acknowledged to recognize the persons and institutions having been involved in transferring effects of the reform policy in Prussia to The Netherlands. Following from this information, especially Johan Rudolph Thorbecke (1798–1872) should be considered (Art. Thorbecke, in: dtv Lexikon, 22, p. 60). After studies and publishing activities in Germany Thorbecke acted as an academic Professor in Ghent and Leyden, but then turned to politics; he became leader of the liberal party and prime minister, even for several periods, as it is documented in relevant literature mentioned below. Gerrit Meijer concluded: "With regard to education policy the educational system was organized in a similar way as proposed by Humboldt" (e-mail of June 28, 2012). Such "similar way" may be found in Kossmann's basic book on the history of the Low Countries 1780–1940 (Kossmann 1978: The Low Countries 1780–1940, Oxford University Press 1978, repr. 1988). For example, in the chapter on "Liberalism as a System, 1948–1978" Kossmann exposed attempts to bring about reforms of the education system in The Netherlands. A reform of the school system was demanded according to the Prussian system; other reformers demanded, that for each creed—or at least for Protestant and Roman Catholic—it should be possible "to be instructed in the seclusion of its own school paid for by the state" (Kossmann 1978, repr. 1988, p. 291). Furthermore, Kossmann referred to Thorbecke, who also argued in favor of reforms of the school system. In Thorbecke's view "Freedom was the main thing and he hoped that the state would gradually be able to withdraw from the field of education." Instead, he had to accept a compromise according to which the state continued "to take care of popular education" (Kossmann 1978, repr. 1988, p. 291). Herewith, it becomes obvious, that the attempts to reform the education system were interlinked with religious movements and changes of the social structure, not in The Netherlands alone.

Concerning the relevant literature apart from Kossmann's work some other studies listed by Gerrit Meijer should be considered: B.H. Slicher van Bath et al. (eds):

Acta Historiae Neerlandicae. Studies on the History of The Netherlands, VII, The Hague (1974) Martinus Nijhoff; I. Hasenberg Butter: *Academic Economics in Holland 1800–1870*, The Hague (1969) Martinus Nijhoff. In these books it becomes obvious, that a basic problem of cultural policy was based on the different concepts of theology and philosophy on the status of the individual and society. This idea was also pointed out by Gerrit Meijer (e-mail of June 2012).

4 The Professionalization of University Studies Since the End of the Twentieth Century

4.1 Long-term Changes of the Framework Conditions of German Universities

The long-term development of German universities as basic component of the system of schooling, cultural education, and scientific research is demonstrated by different characteristics:

1. The history of universities, understood as academic institutions to take care of all disciplines of sciences, may be explained in two ways: (a) as effects of political events and as impact on state, culture, and society or (b) as expression of mental movements, which characterize the mental history of the tradition of the society (Schelsky 1963, p. 13).
2. The "autonomy of the university" was a characteristic feature of universities, which were established in Italy and France during the twelfth and thirteenth century; during later centuries, especially at the twentieth century in Germany, the autonomy was restricted or even excluded. Since the beginning of the twenty-first century new attempts have been made to reinforce the "autonomy of the university" by the state (Hofmann 1968/1969, p. 9 ff).
3. Humboldt's reform of the schooling and education system in Prussia at the beginning of the nineteenth century is part of the long-term changes of the framework conditions fo German universities, though Humboldt's original objectives—diversity ("Mannigfaltigkeit"), individual freedom and independent development—have been interpreted differently and adapted to the political objectives. Since the beginning fo the twenty-first century a "new striving for autonomy of the universities" is proclaimed as a basic objective of public cultural policy, especially concerning the universities. It is also a guideline for the university management by the presidents or rectors and for the administration of the universities in Germany.
4. "Striving for truth" has been a strong motive to establish new universities. During medieval centuries young people wanted to escape social force and barriers of the social groups. In the twenty-first century, a new conflict became apparent: general education by academic teaching and research at autonomous universities

or practice-oriented, professionalized teaching (and research) at professional colleges and academies. This problem is continuously under discussion on all levels of the cultural policy and of the education system.

4.2 *Professionalization of University Studies or Research-oriented University-education?*

The development of universities and specialized academies and professional colleges (Fachhochschulen) in Germany after the Second World War was determined by the demand to rebuild the academic institutions and to start again the lectures and research activities in the available buildings. Four phases of adapting the academic institutions to the changed framework conditions concern: (1) the orientation of the reconstruction process along Humboldt's ideal of academic education (Bildungsideal) (1945–1958), (2) the intensified expansion of universities, academies, and colleges (1958–1969), (3) the phase of take-off and reforms (1968–1970), and (4) the intensively organized institutional changes of the academic sector (universities, academies, and professional colleges), including increased interventions by the state into the academic sector (Boehm et al. 1986, blocks (Spalten), 1301 f). But the development of the academic institutions did not correspond totally to Humboldt's basic concept of academic teaching and research; yet, it should refer to the objectives of the education system: "mass-universities" should prepare large numbers of students for changing or new professions, which depend on new knowledge and scientific education, following from increased technical and organizational progress. Herewith the conflict between Humboldt's ideal of general education orientated to freedom and independence of individuals and the demand for practice-oriented ("anwendungsorientierte") academic teaching and research according to new principles of university education became obvious. To solve this conflict, combinations of general and specialized/professionalized institutions of education were proposed. The result should be exposed by a system of differentiated institutions of general and professionalized education (Boehm et al. 1986, blocks (Spalte), p. 1301).

Considering the present problems of German universities facing the changed framework conditions, the obligations of universities, academies, and professional colleges (Fachhochschulen) should be more precisely defined. The contents of the studies—the curricula and modules—must be coordinated in the diverse academic institutions, and a more intensive cooperation of these institutions turns out to be strictly necessary. As a result of the coordination and adaptation process focusing on all levels of the system of academic education, relevant new paths toward an efficient reorganization of universities, academies, and professional colleges (Fachhochschulen) may be verified. The cultural policy, especially on the level of universities and professional colleges should be able to arrange the adequate structure of the cooperation. The involved academic institutions will also find solutions to integrate teaching and research—pure scientific research at universities and academies, applied scientific teaching and research at professional colleges—and to develop the adequate system of academic institutions under consideration, but simultaneously under modification of Humboldt's basic concept of schooling and academic education.

Examples of integrated studies based on pure and applied scientific research were developed in Germany by new academic institutions: They were established in North Rhine-Westphalia since 1972 as "Gesamthochschulen" (Rau 1977), but they were reorganized to function as universities since 1992, not disregarding Humboldt's basic objectives: "Mannigfaltigkeit" of studies and "individuelle Freiheit und Selbständigkeit" of the individual, but also of social groups and of the society.

5 Conclusions

1. The long-term development of institutions of higher education, especially of universities was charaterized by periods of stagnation, followed by periods of reforms (Hofmann 1968/1969). Every reform should bring about new knowledge, which was opposed to the existing, but decaying level of knowledge about "truth."
2. The universities were established in earlier centuries as autonomous institutions, but they were restricted by political and economic changes during later centuries.
3. Two examples of German students of the eighteenth century—Karl August von Hardenberg and Wilhelm von Humboldt—let conclude, that the universities were characterized by few faculties, by lack of coordination of curricula, by students deciding on their time to be spent for studies or leisure, and by professors preferring to hold small seminars with few students than to offer lectures in front of large numbers of students; moreover, the students (especially of nobility) were not obliged to pass a final exam; Hardenberg and Humboldt proved it.
4. The modern universities at the beginning of the twenty-first century are determined by changed framework conditions and adaption processes, including the increased impact of professionalization of the academic education.
5. The comparison of Humboldt's basic concept of the foundation of universities and of the related concept at the beginning of the twenty-first century demonstrates:

   - The professionalization of teaching at the modern university characterizes the present and future academic education at the university;
   - The universities and other institutions of academic education are characterized by heterogeneity ("Mannigfaltigkeit") and search for truth ("Wahrheitssuche"), but interventions by the state have been of strong influence on the organization of teaching and research.
   - There is a direct link from Humboldt's ideal of university education and the studies carried out in modern universities, academies, and professional colleges ("Fachhochschulen"): heterogeneity of studies and research disciplines, but interventions by the state in order to strengthen the efficiency of teaching and research by new legislation on universities and on academic institutions to be founded in the near future.

References

Boehm, L., Karpen, U., & Finkenstaedt, T. (1986). Hochschulen. In *Staatslexikon* (7th ed., Vol. 2, pp. 1296–1312) Freiburg: Herder Verlag ed. by Görres-Gesellschaft.

Busch, U. (2005). *Die Rolle des Konflikts Hardenberg—Wilhelm von Humboldt beim Scheitern der Verfassungsreform in Preußen. Studienarbeit.* München: GRIN-Verlag für akademische Texte.

Deutscher Taschenbuch Verlag. (2006). dtv-Lexikon (Vol. 22), Wissen Media Verlag GmbH, Gütersloh/München.

Duchhardt, H. (2010). *Freiherr vom Stein. Preußens Reformer und seine Zeit.* München: C. H. Beck-Verlag, Beck'sche Reihe/C. H. Beck-Wissen.

Fisch, E. & Vollmer, H. (1998). Einblicke—Ausblicke. 25 Jahre Universität Paderborn Gesamthochschule, hrsg. im Auftrag des Rektorates der Universität-GH Paderborn, Paderborn.

Gall, L. (2011). *Wilhelm von Humboldt. Ein Preuße von Welt.* Berlin: Propyläen Verlag/Ullstein Buchverlage GmbH.

Gerber, H. (1959). Universitäten und Hochschulen. In *Handwörterbuch der Sozialwissenschaften* (Vol. 10, pp. 471–479). Stuttgart: Verlag Gustav Fischer (ed. by E. v. Beckerath et al.).

Hasenberg, B. I. (1969). *Academic Economics in Holland 1800–1870*, The Hague: Martinus Nijhoff.

Hermann, I. (2003). *Hardenberg. Der Reformkanzler*. Berlin: Siedler Verlag.

Hofmann, W. (1968/1969). *Universität, Ideologie, Gesellschaft. Beiträge zur Wissenschaftssoziologie*. (3 ed.). Frankfurt a. M: Suhrkamp.

Klausa, G. -A. (1990). *Friedrich Karl von Hardenberg (1696–1763). Ein hannoverscher Hofmann und Staatsdiener im Zeitalter der Aufklärung*. Hildesheim: Verlag August Lax.

Kossmann, E. H. (1978). *The low countries 1780–1940*. Oxford: Oxford University Press. (reprint 1988).

Rau, J., et al. (1977). Fünf Jahre Gesamthochschulen in Nordrhein-Westfalen. Bilanz der Gründungsphase, Düsseldorf.

Schelsky, H. (1963). Einsamkeit und Freiheit, Idee und Gestalt der deutschen Universität und ihrer Reformen. Rowohlt, Reinbek bei Hamburg.

Slicher van Bath, B. H., et al. (Eds.). (1974). *Acta Historiae Neerlandicae. Studies on the History of The Netherlands, VII*. The Hague (Martinus Nijhoff).

Stamm-Kuhlmann, Th. (ed.) (2000). Karl August von Hardenberg 1750–1822. Tagebücher und autobiographische Aufzeichnungen, Harald Boldt Verlag im R. Oldenbourg Verlag, München.

von Bothmer, W., & Köhler, M. (Hrsg.). (2011). *Im Auftrag der Krone: Friedrich Karl von Hardenberg und das Leben in Hannover um 1750*. Rostock: Hinstorff Verlag GmbH.

Weber, M. (1922). *Gesammelte Aufsätze zur Wissenschaftslehre*. Tübingen: Verlag J. C. B. Mohr (Paul Siebeck).

Wikipedia. (2012). http://de.wikipedia.org/wiki/Wilhelm_von_Humboldt. Accessed 23 Feb 2012.

The University: Idea and Practice

Gerrit Meijer

1 Introduction

On May 26, 1988 a dissertation with statements was defended at the University of Groningen, The Netherlands. The first statement (Meijer 1988) by the young doctor—and therefore in his view the most important—was:

The science policy in The Netherlands is pervaded by a spirit of fabrilism, which misunderstands the nature and task of the university, and therefore forms in increasing measure a threat to academic freedom.

A spirit of fabrilism can approximately be described as a technocratic spirit. The term is taken from K. J. Popma (1969, pp. 9–11).[1]

The dissertation—on Neoliberalism (1988)—and the statements were after defense accepted by the Faculty and in this way the present writer became on that day a doctor in the economic sciences.

During my study at the University in Groningen (September 1958 to February 1964) I followed the facultative lectures in philosophy of Prof. Dr. Klaas Johan Popma (1903–1986) (on Friday afternoon for 3 h: 1 h Introduction, 1 h Capita Selecta, and 1 h Ethics (four to seven o' clock).

Popma was an extraordinary (*bijzonder*) professor appointed by the private Society for Calvinistic Philosophy (*Vereniging voor Calvinistische Wijsbegeerte*), nowadays renamed as Society for Christian Philosophy. On Calvinist Philosophy: See especially Dooyeweerd (1997), Marlet (1954), and Popma (1956).

[1] Het wetenschapsbeleid in Nederland is doortrokken van een geest van fabrilisme, die de aard en functie van de universiteit miskent, en vormt daarom in toenemende mate een bedreiging voor de academische vrijheid.Een geest van fabrilisme is bij benadering te omschrijven als een technocratische geest. De term is ontleend aan K.J. Popma, De universiteit: idee en praktijk, Amsterdam: Buijten en Schipperheijn 1969, pp. 9–11.

G. Meijer (✉)
University of Maastricht, Larixlaan 3, 1231 BL Loosdrecht, The Netherlands
e-mail: g.meijer@hetnet.nl

J. G. Backhaus (ed.), *The University According to Humboldt*,
SpringerBriefs in Economics 89, DOI 10.1007/978-3-319-13856-5_6

My statement on the university was inspired by the lectures of Popma, and more in particular by his small booklet on The University: Idea and Practice (1969), and my experiences in particular at the University of Amsterdam in the years 1967–1989 (De Jong 1981).

The background of the statement will be discussed in this essay. Therefore, the main features of the study of Popma will be discussed in Sect. 2–4. In Sect. 5 some attention will be paid to developments in science policy in The Netherlands, in the years after 1988, in particular during the time I was employed at the University of Maastricht (1989–2003) and some concluding remarks are given.

2 Popma on the University: Idea and Practice

The study was written as a reaction to the note written by Prof. Dr. Kees Posthumus (1902–1972) professor in general chemistry at the Technical High School Eindhoven in his dignity of government commissioner (*regeringscommissaris*) for scientific education on The University: objectives, functions, structures (in Dutch K. Posthumus (1968), *De universiteit: doelstellingen, functies, structuren, Voorlichtingsdienst OKW, Staatsdrukkerij te 's Gravenhage.*)

According to the writer (Posthumus) and the Minister of Education (Dr. Gerard Heinrich Veringa, 1924–1999) it was meant as a note for discussion:

"Every form of one-sided pressure for reform would do damage to the essence of the university," writes Veringa in the Preface.[2]

Although the Minister uses here the term "essence" of the university the brochure is not about the idea and history of the university. It is only on the practice: the objectives, the functions, the structures. Nothing is said about the history and idea of the university. The university is not treated in its cultural context. This is according to Popma the working-method of the *Homo faber*.

The university originates already in antiquity. The history goes back far beyond the late Middle Ages. In antiquity university means *universitas scientiarum, the coherence of the sciences.* The medieval university is an *universitas magistrorum et scolarium*, i.e. a community of teachers *and* pupils. This is the same principle.

According to Popma, the university of today is not a university, but degenerated to a multiversity, and is only administratively united as a bundle of professional schools (*Fachschulen*). It only has the name: university.

Fabrilism is a principle and radical misjudgment of the human nature. The crisis of the university is the degeneration into an administratively united bundle of professional, special sciences. The fabrilist only puts the question: How are you doing that? Not the question: What in the end am I doing? For this last question the student needs to be educated in the history and philosophy of his science, in order

[2] Elke vorm van eenzijdige hervormingsdrang zou het wezen van de universiteit slechts schade berokkenen" (Posthumus, Preface, 1968, p. 2).

not to become a fabrilist. Both questions have to be combined in order to hold free the road for humanity and freedom.

3 The Idea of Fabrilism

In order to make the idea of fabrilism more clear, Popma refers to the French philosopher Henri Bergson (1895–1941). Bergson (1941, 12th edition: 91 f) distinguishes *H. faber, Homo sapiens*, and *Homo loquax*. He writes:

We believe that it is the essence of men to create materially and morally, to make things and to form himself. *H. faber*, that is the definition we propose. The *H. sapiens* born out of the reflection of the *H. faber* on his production seems us also worth recognition because he solves by pure intelligence the problems. In the choice of problems a philosopher can be mistaken, another philosopher can correct him; both have done their utmost; both can deserve our recognition and our admiration. *Homo faber, H. sapiens*, for the one and the other, who have the tendency to coincide, we bend. The only one who is antipathetic is *l'Homo loquax*, whose thinking, when he thinks, is only a reflection on his words.[3]

According to Bergson the essence of men is to create materially and morally. This is explained as fabricate, to make things and to form yourself. He is *H. faber*. What, however, happens here to the word *fabriquer*? First he uses the term create, then it is substituted with the word *fabriquer*. Further he talks about to make things (*fabriquer des choses*) and to form yourself (*de fabriquer lui-même*). The meaning of the term *fabriquer* in the first sense is, however, wholly different from the latter.

The question whether academic teaching is training or education, is according to Popma a false problem. Training has always an educative element; education is always an aspect of training. There is a subject–subject relation not a subject–object relation between teacher and student. Although, it is often tried to treat him as an object, e.g., in slave trade, in slavery, in the military system, especially in war (Popma 1968, pp. 38–43), the free and responsible human being by definition is never an object.

Popma prefers not to use the term essence of the university. He prefers to speak of behavior, structure, own character. He sees dehumanization and demonization in the university of today.

---

[3] Nous croyons qu'il est de l'essence de l'homme de créer matériellement et moralement, de fabriquer des choses et de se fabriquer lui-même. Homo faber, telle est la définition que nous proposons. L'Homo sapiens, né de la réflexion de l'Homo faber sur sa fabrication, nous paraît tout aussi digne d'estime tant qu'il résout par la pure intelligence les problèmes qui ne dépendent que d'elle: dans le chois de ces problèmes un philosophe peut se tromper, un autre philosophe le détrompera; tous deux auront travaillé de leur mieux; tous deux pourront mériter notre reconnaissance et notre admiration. Homo faber, Homo sapiens, devant l 'un et l'autre, qui tendent d'ailleurs a se confondre ensemble, nous nous inclinons. Le seul qui nous soit antipathique est l'Homo loquax, don't la pensée, quand il pense, n'est qu'une réflexion sur sa parole (Bergson 1941, 91f).

4 Can the University which is in Crisis Be Saved and Transmitted to the Future?

Popma turns to the question whether the university which is in crisis can be saved and transmitted to the future. To answer this question he refers to the work of the German philosopher Karl Jaspers (1883–1969), in particular his lectures on *Erneuerung der Universität*, 1945, and *Vom lebendigen Geist der Universität*, 1946, both reprinted in *Rechenschaft und Ausblick*, 1958, pp. 161–173; 186–217.

In the nineteenth century, according to Jaspers (1958, p. 171), the university lost its unity. Moreover the university was unable to include technology into the university. There is no cohesion. There are tensions in the university. He writes on the polarity between theology and philosophy:

The whole of the university, however, in all faculties could live in the deep tension between theology and philosophy, which, both to one and other, in their polarity are allies as well as adversaries.[4]

Jaspers gives theology the highest place in the building of the unified system of sciences of the university. Philosophy gets a subordinate place.

Popma (1969, p. 40) digresses on the relation of theology and philosophy as seen by Aristotle and Augustine. He observes that Petrus Damiani (1007–1072) is probably the first who has used the term: *philosophia ancilla theologiae*. The idea however can already be found in Augustine. Popma argues that this tension can be softened by the insight that there has not to be an *ancilla* (a slave), because this is in glaring contradiction with the idea of the university. Otherwise dehumanization and depersonalization will be the consequence.

In this respect he raises the question of the possibility of the confessional university. When in such a university the primacy is given to a theology than this leads in principle to the possibility that this is the end of the university, because all other faculties are subjected to theology. However, a so-called neutral university has also its confession: neutralism.

Besides this point, four other fundamental questions are also discussed: Self-management, democratization, theory of science and debate on foundations, serious amateurism.

Self-management (autonomy) of the university is implied by its nature. However, now fabrilism is penetrating the management of the university more and more. The managers are more and more technocrats and not scientists. Most of them are according to Popma "clever boys, they do not care for science" (1969, p. 66).[5]

"Democratization" (say). Students and "lower" staff ask for more influence. They feel that decisions are made over and without them on the form and content of study and research. This is difficult with nowadays large numbers of students and teachers, but a regular discussion between the members of the university community

[4] Das Ganze der Universität aber in allen Fakultäten konnte leben in der tiefen Spannung von Theologie und Philosophie, die, beide aufeinander angewiesen, in ihrer Polarität ebenso Bundesgenossen wie Gegensätze sind (Jaspers 1958, p. 190).

[5] "Veeleer zijn het handige jongens, de wetenschap kan hen gestolen worden" (p. 66).

on the why and how of university studies and research is needed. This means, that is, to say: what today is called say of students, belongs historically and ideally to the essence of the university (Popma 1969, p. 19).[6] The university is a community of teachers *and* students. The system of one man one vote, however, goes too far. It is excluding or in any case diminishing to an unacceptable level the influence of the teachers in the teaching and research process.

Theory of science and debate on foundations. Some more or less tinkering on the organization does not solve the problem. Every member of the university has to be open for dialog and to take part in it. This means that by all concerned has to exist lively interest for the building of the *unified system of sciences* and *the question of the place of the own discipline*. This calls for distance to one's own discipline. This debate is possible on the foundation of solidarity between people. The solidarity of people in every field of culture is the foundation on which the university according to its idea is built. They have to behave as human beings and in the idea as well in practice not to allow fabrilization, depersonalization, and dehumanization.

The unity of the university, which is demanded by her idea, is only possible along the road of *serious amateurism*. The term has as its stem: *amare*, which is to love. The time is long ago that it was possible to be a universal scholar, like for example Leibniz (1646–1716). Even in his case it is doubted that he reached a universal knowledge of science. This is not only the case with regard to special sciences, but also within them. Moreover it is not possible to control everything one finds in the studies of other scientists. Often it has to be taken for granted. Trust belongs to the nature of the university, and related to solidarity, is necessary to make progress.

To get insight in the idea of the university and the meaning of a special science is only possible in amateurish ways. Popma argues that these are not only desirable; they are inevitable.

5 Concluding Remarks

The study of Popma gives a profound analysis of the way in which fabrilistic thinking on the university has brought it more and more in crisis since about 1850. The diagnosis leads also to the formulation of correct principles for reform. Four of these principles are mentioned: a unified system of sciences (no hierarchy in sciences, neither theology nor philosophy, or whatever); autonomy (self-management of the university); voice (say) for all persons belonging to the university community; serious amateurism (as counter weight of scientific *hybris*). They can be applied as standards for what is healthy or unhealthy. The standards show the tensions between idea and pratice.

The university has to be free from church, state, and any other institution or ideology, and to be autonomous and to belong to the state-free sphere. This was also

[6] "Dat wil zeggen: wat men tegenwoordig de ïnspraak van studenten"noemt, behoort zowel historisch en ideëel tot het meest eigenlijk wezen van de universiteit. (p. 19).

the idea behind the Free University of Amsterdam. In 1880, it started as a private association, free from the state and free of the church. However, already in 1905 it became 95 % financed by the state. Now in fact it cooperates with the University of Amsterdam.

In The Netherlands, universities were founded at the end of the sixteenth century, in the time of the Reformation during The Republic. In the beginning of the nineteenth century The Netherlands became a kingdom. The policy with regard to academic education was influenced mainly by the developments in Germany, among them Humboldt. The Dutch politician Johan Rudolph Thorbecke (1798–1872), who contributed to the organization of education in The Netherlands, agreed with Humboldt on the limits of state action with regard to religion and morals. According to Humboldt "particularly all special supervision of education, religion, sumptuary laws, etc., lies wholly outside the limits of its legitimate activity" (Humboldt 1969, p. 69, 81). In the second half of the twentieth century the orientation changed. The German model was, according to De Jong in the 1960s and 1970s of the twentieth century transformed to the Anglo-Saxon model (De Jong, p. 386). Via the supervision of the central state on means and subsidies; the shortening of curricula; open and disguised reorganizations, etc. the freedom of study and research was infringed upon. The situation has further deteriorated since 1988.

There are and have, however, always been niches in the university and there is plenty of room outside the State-controlled universities for independent scientific education and research. There are famous thinkers who never got tenure, e.g. Baruch Spinoza (1632–1677). During the Nazi-period many scientists decided to leave or had to leave Germany (e.g., Wilhelm Röpke). Others did go in inner emigration or were fired (e.g., Jaspers). After the Nazi seizure of power in 1933, Jaspers was considered to have a "Jewish taint" (*jüdische Versippung*, in the jargon of the time) due to his Jewish wife, and was forced to retire from teaching in 1937. In 1938, he fell under a publication ban as well. Many of his long-time friends stood by him, however, and he was able to continue his studies and research without being totally isolated. But he and his wife were under constant threat of removal to a concentration camp until March 30, 1945, when Heidelberg was liberated by American troops. Jaspers wrote extensively on the threat to human freedom posed by modern science and modern economic and political institutions. Jaspers valued humanism and the continuity of integral cultural traditions in political spheres. He strongly opposed totalitarian despotism and warned about the increasing tendency toward technocracy, or a regime that regarded humans as mere instruments of science and ideological goals. He was also skeptical of majoritarian democracy. Thus, he supported a form of governance that guaranteed individual freedom and limited government yet was rooted in authentic tradition and guided by an intellectual elite.[7] Popma himself was appointed by a private society at the fringe of the State University of Groningen and Utrecht.

At October 17, 2003 the present writer had the opportunity to reflect on some experiences during his working life. With regard to the University of Maastricht

[7] Wikipedia, the free encyclopedia, http://en.wikipedia.org/wiki/Karl_Jaspers

he remarked, that thanks to his transfer in 1989 from the University of Amsterdam to the University of Limburg it became possible for him to shift and broaden his area of teaching and research in a new refreshing environment. The experience in Amsterdam as an economist in teaching students in political science and sociology could now be used in the Section Economics of the Public Sector of the Vakgroep Economics in a Faculty of Economics. There it came to a fruitful way of co-operation with Prof. Dr. Jürgen Backhaus. With much pleasure he looks back to the discussions with the participants in the Brown Bag, which gave the possibility during more than 10 years to work in breadth and depth. Not only the input but also the output of the section gave him much satisfaction. Here was done in the field of research and teaching what may be expected of an academic institution. Here his ideal, as expressed in his statements VII and XI (Meijer 1998)[8], was approached. Parts of the efforts were the Law and Economics Workshop and the Heilbronn Symposion. Both were held in 2012 for the 25th time. They both were organized by Prof. Backhaus.

References

Bergson, H. (1941), *12, La pensée et le mouvant.* Paris: P.U.F.

De Jong, F. (Ed.). (1981). *Macht en Inspraak, De strijd om de democratisering van de universiteit van Amsterdam.* Baarn: ANBO

Dooyeweerd, H. (1997) *A new critique of theoretical thought* (Vols. 1–4). Lewiston: Edwin Mellen Press.

Humboldt, W. von. (1969). *The limits of state action*, Indianapolis: Liberty Fund.

Jaspers, K. (1947). *Die Erneuerung der Universität*, Berlin-Heidelberg-New York: Springer Verlag

Jaspers, K. (1958). *Rechenschaft und Ausblick. Reden und Aufsätze.* München: Piper Verlag

Marlet, M. J. F. (1954). *Grundlinien der Kalvinistischen " Philosophie der Gesetzesidee" als Christlicher Tanszendentalphilosophie*, München: Karl Zink Verlag.

Meijer, G. (1988). *Het neoliberalisme. Neoliberalen over economische orde en economische theorie.* Assen/Maastricht: Van Gorcum/van der Vegt. And De stellingen behorend bij het proefschrift Het Neoliberalisme van Gerrit Meijer.

Popma, K. J. (1956). *Inleiding in de Wijsbegeerte.* Kampen: Kok

Popma, K. J. (1968). *Venster op de wereld.* Kampen: Kok

Popma, K. J. (1969). *Universiteit: idee en praktijk.* Amsterdam: Buijten en Schipperheijn

Popma, K. J., *Humanisme en anti-humanisme.*

Posthumus, K. (1968). *De universiteit: doelstellingen, functies en structuren, 's Gravenhage: Voorlichtingsdienst OKW.* 's Gravenhage: Staatsdrukkerij

[8] The other two statements were:VII. It will be favorable to the development of economic science when a less apposed attitude against historical approaches and reflections on other aspects of reality, in particular the ethical aspect.XI. The point of view that the progress of economic science is fostered by differences in opinion (disagreements) between students (practitioners) supposes a sufficient measure of willingness (readiness) to discuss. From the history of economic science in the twentieth century we find that this is not always present. By exaggerating the differences of opinions the progress can be curbed.

Democracy and Education: A History from Ancient Athens

Nicholas C. Kyriazis and Emmanouil Marios L. Economou

1 Introduction

The ancient Greek philosophers and "political scientists" like Plato and Aristotle were well aware that a precondition for the smooth functioning of democracy was the education of its citizens-voters, thus in a sense anticipating the eighteenth century philosophers such as John Steuart Mill and Wilhelm von Humboldt. Plato took a negative view (in his "Politeia," mainly) believing that the mass of the ordinary citizens were not, and could not be well-educated to run a democracy. Thus, in his eyes, democracy was a bad system of government, degenerating into "mob rule." His solution was the ideal model of a society governed by educated specialists, the "philosophers-guardians." Although Aristotle took a milder view, distinguishing between types of democracy, like an "extremist" one (having in mind Athenian democracy during the Peloponnesian War, 431–404 BCE, when it was run by the so-called "demagogues") and a more "moderate" one (having in mind the Athenian democracy of his own times, 403–322 BCE), he also cast doubts about the ability of ordinary citizens-voters to govern themselves. The main issue they raised, was how could a system be run, in which unequal citizens, from the point of view of education, knowledge, ability, morals, etc. had equal political rights.[1] Philosophers such as Plato and Aristotle argued, that it could not, there was no solution to the problem, and thus democracy was a bad political system. However, practicing

[1] An issue faced also by modern democracies: Should for example a football hooligan, or a member of the SS during the Weimar Republic, or "Golden Dawn" Nazi party in modern Greece, who demonstrate violent behavior, and in the last two cases being avowed enemies of democracy, have the same voting right with an "ordinary" citizen? A satisfactory solution was not found then (leading to the fall of the Weimar Republic) nor now.

N. C. Kyriazis (✉) · E. M. L. Economou
Economics Department, University of Thessaly, Korai 43, Volos 383 33, Thessaly, Greece
e-mail: nkyr@uth.gr

E. M. L. Economou
e-mail: emmoikon@uth.gr

J. G. Backhaus (ed.), *The University According to Humboldt*,
SpringerBriefs in Economics 89, DOI 10.1007/978-3-319-13856-5_7

politicians in democratic Athens, like Themistocles, Pericles, and Lycurgus, were to prove them wrong. Modern philosophers such as Goethe, Hölderlin, and Humboldt, representatives of the so-called "neo-humanistic" movement in Germany during the eighteenth century, revived the significance of studying the political functioning of the ancient Athenian democracy. Humboldt wrote in 1807 an essay, "Geschichte des verfalls und untergangs der griechischen freistaaten" by arguing that ancient Greek literature could be used as a bond to reinforce the historical ties between Germans and Hellenes (Greeks) (Benes 2002).

Having in mind Humboldt's works concerning education, liberalism, and ancient Greek literature, we analyze the role of education for the smooth running of the Athenian direct democracy through the use of the period's mass media, theatrical plays, and through participation in the popular Assembly itself. The essay is organized as follows: First, we present a model of "macrocultures," that illustrate change from a previous (aristocratic, oligarchic, or tyrannical) political system to a democratic one, taking as a case study the emergence of democracy in ancient Greece. Then, we present some cases in Classical times to show how Athenian "initiators"[2] used education measures to achieve, under direct democracy, specific aims. This is followed by our conclusions.

2 A Model of Macroculture and Change

In this section, we introduce the concept of macroculture (taken over and adapted from organization theory) into institutional economics in order to analyze structural change. A "macroculture" encompasses the common values, norms, and beliefs that are being shared among the members of a company, a society, or a state.

Through these values, norms, and beliefs, a macroculture creates typical standards of behavior among independent entities, and coordinates their activities so that complex tasks may be completed (Jones et al. 1997; Abrahamson and Fombrun 1992, 1994). This happens by creating a dynamic environment where colleagues in an association or individuals as members of a social group share broad tacitly understood rules of behavior by undertaking appropriate actions under unspecified contingencies. These common rules of behaviour could also be characterized as "routines" or "special information" about how a policy should be implemented or in what way a problem could be solved (Williamson 1975, 1991; Camerer and Vepsalainen 1988). These ideas are also consistent with Lazaric (2011, p. 148), who claims that "every recurrent interaction pattern in an organization may be hiding a potential routine." Then, the establishment of "communication protocols" follows. This means, that each sub-group of a company or society should establish efficient

[2] We prefer the term "initiator" than politician to characterize leaders of ancient Athens, since at the time, there were not established political parties, and most government positions were covered by lot. The initiators brought forward initiatives in front of the citizens Assembly, and arguing in order to convince citizens to vote in favor.

ways of collaborating and sharing information and ideas with the other groups, easily and fast. It is obvious that the faster the information is shared among subgroups, the more the transactional cost for a company or a society is diminishing as a whole.

Jones et al. (1997), O'Neil et al. (2004), and Lawrence and Philips (2004) have applied this concept of macroculture to firms, while Almond and Verba (1963) parallel this, writing on "civic culture" as a shared set of beliefs among citizens. Moreover, Putnam (1993) argues that democratic stability depends on specific forms of social organization and citizen values which he calls "civic traditions," while in a similar line of argumentation Granovetter (1992, p. 35) argues that firms develop connected mutual contacts to one another. This leads to the establishment of mutual links or networks. These interactions define values and norms and thus strengthen this interdependence, the macroculture.

Two particular questions on this issue are, first how a macroculture develops and why are macrocultures proceeding along different paths, evolving different characteristics, e.g., what are the causes that shape macrocultures. Related to this is the issue of "cause" and effect. Do values and norms preexists (and if so, why and how did they come about) and do they shape a particular macroculture, or is it the other way round, that is, a macroculture gives rise to specific values and norms. Thus, an actual answer can be given only if we manage to establish chronological sequences of events.[3]

The other important issue concerning macroculture, in our adaptation of the term in economics, society, and politics, has to do with its dynamic characteristic: we are referring to a process where the interaction of values or sets of behavior lead finally to the creation of new values or institutions which result to a dynamic process of a social, political, or an economic regime change.

For example, Kyriazis and Paparrigopoulos (2011) and Kyriazis (2012) have analyzed one aspect of macroculture, which has to do with the emergence of a new type warrior in Archaic pre-classical Greece, the "hoplite" (named from his big round shield, the "hoplon") and the new tactical formation, the "phalanx," as coordination and cooperation mechanisms which give rise to specific mental attitudes, values, and norms, even a specific language (e.g., clear commands for battle) learning and knowledge. Even more, the new warship adopted during the early fifth century by the Greeks, the "trireme" and the naval fleets, developed and fine-tuned cooperation and coordination mechanisms in the phalanx "customs" values and norms.[4]

Kyriazis and Economou (2014) have analyzed the interaction of a series of values through sports and warfare in pre-Classical Greece, such as courage, trust, equality, coordination, collaboration and concord, etc. that gave a strong stimulus to the emergence of democracy during the fifth century BCE, while in a similar research Kyriazis and Economou (forthcoming) raised the issue of some other social aspects

[3] This point has been raised as a criticism against North (1981) by Daunton (2010).

[4] For the way that the phalanx formation was deployed in battlefields during war campaigns see Hanson (2009).

during the Classical period (fifth century BCE) such as religion, the protection of property rights and the "proto-democratic" values in pro-Classical Greece, as a way of creation of new values when interacting each other.

In Fig. 1, we represent the different elements of a macroculture (e.g., in athletics, religion, warfare, economy, politics, elements of democratic behavior, etc.) that are gradually being integrated into a new whole: The cycles represent the various elements of a new macroculture that emerges in one sector (e.g., democratic ideals depicted by cycle 1 and values through sports depicted by cycle 2) at time period 1. These values are reinforced through diffusion and interaction with other sectors at periods 2 and 3, and being integrated into a new mutually supporting macroculture at period 4. This is exactly how macrocultures develop and being strengthened and this is what happened in the ancient Athenian democracy.

In the next section, we analyze the democratic macroculture that gradually emerged in Classical Athens by a process of educating people through the speeches of experts in the popular assembly and the theatrical plays.

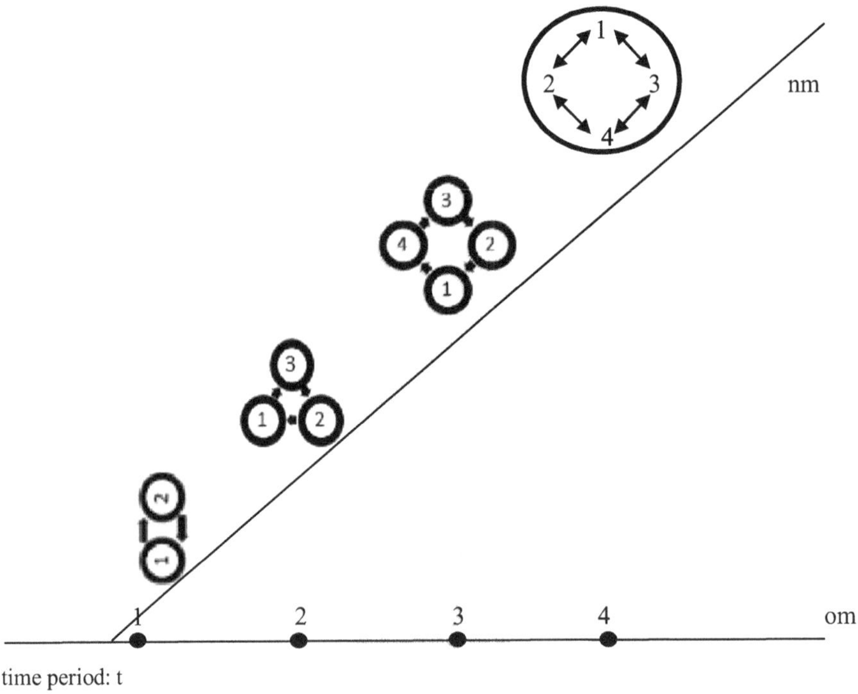

Fig. 1 Integration of various elements of macroculture

3 Democracy and Education in Classical Athens

Even before the criticism put forward by the philosophers, democratic initiators well understood that education of citizens was necessary if correct decisions in the Assembly were to be reached. The practical issue was how could this be achieved, during a period were no compulsory education of children existed, and when children's education was a private family matter. Children of rich families got a good education in reading, writing poetry, music, morals, and religion (after the mid-fifth century also in "rhetoric" and politics). By contrast, children of poor citizens probably got none or they had access on the "basic" (elementary)[5] education, and thus, they were often illiterate. But in ancient democracies, as in modern ones, less well off citizens constituted the great majority.

After the great Athenian victory at Marathon in 490 BCE, Themistocles, foreseeing the danger of the second Persian invasion, initiated his famous proposition, known as "Themistocles Naval Decree or Law" of 483/2 BCE to finance the building of 100 new warships (triremes) each in 2 consecutive years, out of the proceeds of the Lavrion silver mines (Kyriazis and Zouboulakis 2004). At the time a new very rich vein of sylver was discovered. After paying all ordinary budget expenditures, there was still a surplus, and Themistocles opponent, Aristides, who was supported by the aristocratic elite, proposed that the proceeds should be distributed to all 60,000 Athenian citizens, each receiving 10 drachmae (about 15 working days remuneration).[6]

So, the two proposals were: either Aristides', to use the surplus for private consumption, or Themistocles', to use it in order to finance the public good defense (warships). The decision was not easy. How could the Athenians be convinced to forego a "gift" of private consumption in order to acquire a public good? Themistocles undertook to educate the Athenians prior to the vote. His political friends would probably speak informally in every occasion, to groups of their friends and acquaintances, in market places, festivals, dinners (the famous "symposia") making clear the looming Persian danger and the advantages accruing to the simple citizens. The major points would have been, first the safeguard of the city's independence and democracy and second, full political rights for class of poor citizens, called "thetes"[7] (Lyttkens 2013). But for the first time ever, Themistocles used the time's "mass media" to educate his fellow citizens. He entrusted one of his friends, to commission a play, by playwright Phrynichus, a tragic poet, called the "Fall of Miletus,"[8] to be presented during the theatrical contests. The play, illustrating the

[5] For this issue, see Kyriazis and Economou (2013) and the references there in.

[6] For the calculation of the number of the Athenian citizens during the fifth century, being 60,000, see Kyriazis and Paparrigopoulos (2012). The basic source is Herodotus "History."

[7] At the time the fourth class (according to wealth criteria) the "thetes" did not have full political rights. They would vote, but not be elected to government positions (Kyriazis 2012). But by serving as rowers in the fleet, e.g., taking part in the defense of their country, they would get full political rights, as they finally did.

[8] Miletus on the coast of Asia Minor was sacked and destroyed by the Persians in 479 BCE, after the unsuccessful Ionian Revolt against Persian rule.

losses and the hardships of the population after the fall of the city, was a direct warning as to what would happen to the Athenians if they were not successful in facing the Persian invasion, e.g., if they did not accept Themistocles' proposals. Thousands of Athenians saw the play in Attica's theaters. They were moved to tears, and they fined the playwright, because he reminded them the tragic fate of their compatriots in Asia Minor. But they got the educational message. When the time came, they voted in favor of Themistocles proposal, the fleet was build, and the Athenians together with the fleets of some other city-states won the great naval battle of Salamis in 480 BCE. Greece and democracy were saved.[9] It was a triumph of direct democracy and education. Themistocles showed that ordinary citizens could be educated in order to reach correct decisions. But except the educational process, what is also important here, is the fact of the free choice of the Athenian people to decide and support willingly the correct policy, by taking into account the pros and cons. It was a conscious decision taken by the people, who had a very good access to information concerning the real situation and the alternative choices they had to decide on. This idea of freedom of choice to decide whatever you wish was one of the main fundamentals of both Kant's and Humboldt's beliefs (see Rhonheimer 2013, pp. 45–46).

Later Athenian initiators well understood the precedent set by Themistocles. By the second half of the fifth century, the era when Pericles dominated the Athenian political scene, a very important step in education was undertaken: "Theorika," payment to the poorer Athenians out of the state budget, of money in order to allow them to watch the 4 days long theatrical contests. Since they took 4 complete days, if not paid, poor Athenians would lose 4 days remuneration (wages, etc.) which they could ill afford.[10] Thus, the theater became the first state sponsored and publicly financed type of education. Athenian plays teached almost everything: history and mythology (for example, Aeschylus "The Persians" … "The Trojan Women" … "Ajax," the "Seven against Thebes" and "Mycenaean" cycles) religion, morals, politics, and political criticism (as for example, "Antigone,"[11] "Oedipus" the comedies of Aristophanes, etc). Theater plays were not perform only in the city of Athens, but all over the scattered Athenian "deme" (communities) so that the educational teaching reached almost all Athenians.

But apart from the theater, participating in the Assembly meetings, of which about 40 full days long were held during the fourth century per year (Hansen 1999), provided simple Athenians with education. An Athenian citizen who had participated in about half (20 out of 40) annual meetings of the Assembly, after 10 years (when he could have reached his 30th year) he would have heard during 200 meetings the best experts on every subject (foreign policy, strategy, public works, economics, etc.)

[9] Of the 340 Greek ships at Salamis, 180 were Athenian (Strauss 2004; Shepherd 2010).

[10] Contrary to older views, modern scholars have presented a lot of evidence that the average Athenian citizen was hard working, either as self-employed in one of the almost 200 types of jobs specified by Xenophon on "Oeconomicus" and "Cyropaedia," or as a salaried employee (Cohen 1992; Amemiya 2007; Halkos and Kyriazis 2010).

[11] On morals, Antigone includes the famous line "I was not born to hate but to love," a precursor by five centuries of Christian teaching.

arguing in favor or against a plethora of issues. Having heard of them, he would have become a well-informed citizen-voter, with considerable knowledge on all public subjects. Listening and being guided by the experts in the Assembly, created common knowledge, commitment, and facilitated coordination and cooperation in the political field (Ober 2008, Chap. 5).[12]

Again, Athenian initiators well understood that for the good working of the Athenian direct democracy, poorer Athenian citizens would have to be enabled to participate. To make this possible, they adopted a similar solution to that for watching the theater performances. They paid to the first 6000 citizens to attend the Assembly (6000 being the required quorum) a sum for their attendance, to be paid again out of the state's budget, called "eklesiastika" (Kyriazis 2009).[13]

As a final comment in this session, it could be said that the values and principles that were developed through theatrical plays, such as moral behavior, valor, integrity of character, personal pride, etc. were also correlated with values expressed through the democratic assembly of citizens, reinforcing thus a wider democratic macroculture that had to do with society as a whole, instead of being a privilege of the intellectuals or the high ranking officials of the state. Figure 2 is a simple depiction of this relationship of the emerging democratic values through the popular assembly and theatrical plays:

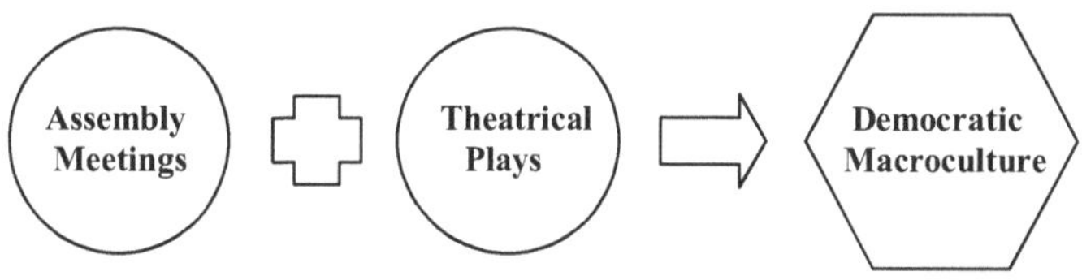

Fig. 2 The democratic macroculture and education

[12] We have argued (Kyriazis 2012; Kyriazis and Metaxas 2013) that ancient Greeks developed coordination and cooperation mechanisms, which were the phalanx tactical formation, and the ships (triremes) and fleets. Values and norms developed in the military field, like equality, self-awareness, listening to the expert, courage, etc., were taken over and adapted as democratic political values. For example, it required real political courage (known as "paressia"), to come confidently forward in the Assembly and make specific proposals, as the initiator could face substantial punishments if his proposal proved to be wrong, mainly fines, but sometimes even the death penalty. The victor of Marathon, Miltiades was fined to the exorbitant fine of 50 talents for his failed military expedition against Paros, which his son Kimon paid after his death.

[13] "Eklesia" being the name of the popular Assembly, originally meaning coming together, gathering. The name was taken over in Greek and Latin to mean religious gatherings, in Christian times, church. The remuneration was between 4 and 6 obols, 1 drachma being 6 obols and 1 drachma being the average wage for skilled worker during the second half of the fifth century. This was the wage paid to workers (stone masons, etc.) in the Acropolis-Parthenon building project.

4 Conclusion

We have sketched above, for the first time as far as we know, the role of education for the smooth running of the Athenian direct democracy. Similar policies were adopted also by other Greek democracies, although we are better informed about Athens due to a wealth of extant sources. Athenian initiators and orators understood well that democracy can be as good or as bad as its citizens, so they tried to educate them. They introduced two ingenious policy measures: Education through the use of the period's mass media, theatrical plays, and through participation in the Assembly itself. To allow poorer citizens to participate, they gave them incentives, in the form of "participation fees." Lack of interest in modern democracies of citizens to participate in elections (even if held every 4 or 5 years) is increasing in Europe. This again is linked to problems with the functioning of democracy, rise of extremist parties, "euroscepticism," etc. Can we learn something from ancient democracy? Can we educate today's citizen's for them to be more interested, better informed to become more conscious and "better" democrats? Athenian experience indicates that the introduction of direct democracy procedures like popular initiatives leading to referenda with binding results does motivate citizens more, and gives them more knowledge on the particular issues, thus educating them politically.

Public education is now of course obligatory and paid in part out of the state's budget, a culmination of the first steps taken by the Athenians through "theorika." But the main issue here concerns the content of public education: Modern children, up to the time they finish university studies as adults get a lot of information on very varied subjects but the main questions are still pertinent: Do they get an education that will make them better citizens and democrats? This is of course an ongoing discussion on educational aims, teaching methods, etc., but a general answer seems to indicate that democracies are not working better during recent years, and that democratization is falling back, a very disturbing trend.[14] What is not in doubt is the importance of education for forging a democratic macroculture between people in the European Union. The fourth century BCE Athenian orator Demades, being perfectly aware of this, remarked that "theorika" was the "glue of democracy" (Plut. Mor. 1016B). We are convinced that Humboldt would fully concur.

Bibliography

Ancient Authors

Herodotus "History". (Hist.).
Plutarch "Morallia". (Mor.).
Xenophon "Oeconomicus". (Oe.).
Xenophon "Cyropaedia". (C.).

[14] According to the "Freedom in the World" indicator for 2014, there is an erosion in global freedom, with 54 countries registering declines and 40 gains.

Modern Authors

Abrahamson, E., & Fombrun, C. J. (1992). Forging the iron cage: Interorganisational networks and the production of macro-culture. *Journal of Management Studies, 29,* 175–194.

Abrahamson, E., & Fombrun, C. J. (1994). Macrocultures: Determinants and consequences. *Academy of Management Review, 19*(4), 728–755.

Almond, G. A., & Verba, S. (1963). *The civic culture: Political attitudes and democracy in five nations*. California: Sage (reprinted 1989).

Amemiya, T. (2007). *Economy and economics in ancient Greece*. London: Routledge.

Benes, K. E. (2002). Linguistic history and memories of national origin 1806–1815. In C. Emden & D. Midgley (Eds.), *German literature, history and the nation* (pp. 229–253). Bern: P. Lang.

Camerer, C., & Vepsalainen, A. (1988). The economic efficiency of corporate culture. *Strategic Management Journal, 9,* 115–126.

Cohen, E. E. (1992). *Athenian economy and society. A banking perspective*. Princeton: Princeton University Press.

Daunton, M. (2010). Rationality and institutions: Reflections on Douglas North. *Structural Change and Economic Dynamics, 21,* 147–156.

Economou, E. M. L. & Kyriazis, N. (2014). Property rights and democratic values in pre-Classical Greece, *Social Science Tribune*, ΙΣΤ(63): 46–59.

Economou, E. M. L., & Kyriazis, N. (forthcoming, a). Property rights and democratic values in pre-Classical Greece, *Social Science Tribune*.

Freedom House Annual Report. (2014). Freedom in the World Booklet. http://freedomhouse.org/sites/default/files/FIW2014%20Booklet.pdf. Accessed 21 June 2014.

Granovetter, M. (1992). Problems of explanation in economic sociology. In N. Nabria & R. G. Eccles (Eds.), *Networks and organizations: Structure, forms and action* (pp. 25–26). Harvard: Harvard Business School Press.

Halkos G., & Kyriazis, N. (2010). The Athenian economy in the age of Demosthenes, *European Journal of Law and Economics, 29,* 255–277.

Hansen, M. H. (1999). *The Athenian democracy in the age of Demosthenes*. London: Bristol Classical.

Hanson, V. D. (2009). *The western way of war. Infantry battle in Classical Greece*. Berkeley: University of California Press.

Jones, C., Hesterly, W. S., & Borgatti, S. P. (1997). A general theory of network governance: Exchange conditions and social mechanisms. *Academy of Management Review, 22*(4), 911–945.

Kyriazis, N. (2009). Financing the Athenian state: Public choice in the age of Demosthenes. *European Journal of Law and Economics, 27,* 109–127.

Kyriazis, N. (2012). *Why ancient Greece?* Athens: Psychogios.

Kyriazis, N., & Economou, E. M. L. (2013). Macroculture, sports and democracy in Classical Greece, *European Journal of Law and Economics*. doi:10.1007/s10657-013-9390-3.

Kyriazis, N., & Metaxas T. (2013). The emergence of democracy: a behavioural perspective. Munich Personal RePEc Archive, MPRA Paper No. 47146.

Kyriazis, N., & Paparrigopoulos, X. (2011). The birth of democracy: Values in war and politics in Classical Greece. In P. Hermann (Ed.), *Democracy in the theory and action* (pp. 277–287). New York: Nova.

Kyriazis, N., & Paparrigopoulos, X. (2012). War and democracy in ancient Greece. *European Journal of Law and Economics*. doi:10.1007/s10657-012-9352-1.

Kyriazis, N., & Zouboulakis, M. (2004). Democracy, sea power and institutional change: An economic analysis of the Athenian Naval Law. *European Journal of Law and Economics, 17,* 117–132.

Lawrence, T. B., & Phillips, N. (2004). From Moby Dick to Free Willy: Macro-cultural discourse and institutional entrepreneurship in emerging institutional fields, *Organization, 11*(5), 689–711.

Lazaric, N. (2011). Organizational routines and cognition: An introduction to empirical and analytical contributions. *Journal of Institutional Economics, 7*(2), 147–156.

Lyttkens, C. H. (2013). *Economic analysis of institutional change in ancient Greece. Politics, taxation and rational behaviour*. Abingdon: Routledge.

North, D. (1981). *Structure and change in economic history*. New York: W.W. Norton and Company.

Ober, J. (2008). *Democracy and knowledge. Innovation and learning in Classical Athens*. Princeton: Princeton University Press.

O'Neil, J., Beauvais, L. L., & Scholl, R. W. (2004). Strategic issues and determinant factors of an interorganizational macroculture in the lodging industry. *Journal of Hospitality & Tourism Research, 20*(10), 1–24.

Putnam, R. (1993). *Making democracy work*. Princeton: Princeton University Press.

Rhonheimer, M. (2013). *The common good of constitutional democracy: Essays in political philosophy*. Washington D.C.: The Catholic University of America Press.

Shepherd, W. (2010). *Salamis 480 BC. Osprey, Campaign, 222*. Midland: Osprey.

Strauss, B. (2004). *The battle of Salamis: The naval encounter that saved Greece-and western civilization*. New York: Simon and Schuster.

Williamson, O. (1975). *Markets and hierarchies: Analysis and antitrust implications*. New York: Free Press.

Williamson, O. (1991). Comparative economic organization: The analysis of discrete structural alternatives. *Administrative Science Quarterly, 36*(2), 269–296.

MIX
Papier aus verantwortungsvollen Quellen
Paper from responsible sources
FSC® C105338

FSC
www.fsc.org

If you have any concerns about our products,
you can contact us on
ProductSafety@springernature.com

In case Publisher is established outside the EU,
the EU authorized representative is:
Springer Nature Customer Service Center GmbH
Europaplatz 3, 69115 Heidelberg, Germany

Printed by Libri Plureos GmbH
in Hamburg, Germany